ACHIEVE:
Maximize Your Potential with 7 Keys to Unlock Success and Significance

RIA STORY

Some names and identifying details have been changed to protect the privacy of individuals.

Copyright © 2018 Ria Story
All rights reserved.
ISBN: 1548296619

ISBN-13: 978-1548296612

ACHIEVE

DEDICATION

This book is dedicated to those who are ready to maximize their potential in life and leadership. We change the world when we change ourselves.

What Others Are Saying About Ria and Her Books:

"I want to start by saying thank you…You made me want to try at life because you made me realize that you can make it anywhere you want, no matter where or what you are from. THANK YOU SO MUCH!" JONATHAN, HIGH SCHOOL STUDENT

"Ria's book (Beyond Bound and Broken) is full of hope and inspiration, and she shows us that despite experiencing horrific trauma as a young adult, that if we choose to, we can get past anything with the attitude that we bring to our life…Her book is full of wonderful quotes and wisdom."
MADELEINE BLACK, AUTHOR OF UNBROKEN

"I am using your material to empower myself and my female clients. Thanks for sharing your story and a wonderful journey of growth."
SUE QUIGLEY, LICENSED CLINICAL THERAPIST

"Very few 'victims' would be willing to share such a personal story. However, nothing about Ria is average. She chose to rise above her painful past and now positions it in a way to offer hope and healing to others who've been through unspeakable abuse. Ria's faith and marriage keep her grounded as she reveals the solid foundation which helps her stand as an overcomer. Read this story and find yourself and your own story strengthened."
KARY OBERBRUNNER, AUTHOR AND FOUNDER OF AUTHOR ACADEMY ELITE, ON *RIA'S STORY FROM ASHES TO BEAUTY*

"Thank you, Ria, for bringing our conference to a close. You were definitely an inspiration to all of us! Awesome Job!"
MELINDA, PRESIDENT AGS

"Beyond Bound and Broken is a deeply inspirational book; one that will stay with you for years to come. The lessons are deep, yet practical, and her advice leads to clear solutions. This is a profoundly hopeful book. We all face pain, difficulty, and doubt but with resilience, we can lead vital, flourishing lives. Ria's story although sometimes painfully difficult to read because of the trials she endured is a story of great courage and compassion both for herself as victim and for those who betrayed her. Forgiveness is a strong theme as is courage. I would highly recommend this book to anyone who is struggling to move forward after experiencing a great trial." AMAZON CUSTOMER

"…it was awesome! Ria has a real gift. I came away with so many helpful tools! Thank you, Ria."
STEFANIE, CONFERENCE ATTENDEE

"May God continue to bless your efforts. Your triumph is a great joy, and a gift to all that would hear or read it."
LOUIS O., HUMAN RIGHTS ADVOCATE

"What an inspiration you are to all of us especially the women audience. Your book is a clear example & step by step guide on how to become an effective leader. It is so easy to read and simple yet meaningful which is the beauty of this book."
K. POONWALA, CUSTOMER SUCCESS MANAGER, ON *LEADERSHIP GEMS FOR WOMEN*

"I was truly inspired by your presentation and the life lessons taught." JENNIFER, CONFERENCE ATTENDEE

CONTENTS

Introduction i

Key #1: Attitude
1 Attitude Creates Positivity 1
2 Attitude Creates Possibility 5
3 Attitude Creates Perspective 9
4 Attitude Creates Potential 13

Key #2: Choices
5 Choices Today Define How You Go 17
6 Choices Today Define How You Grow 21
7 Choices Today Define How You Can Give 25
8 Choices Today Define How You Will Live 29

Key #3: Humility
9 Humility Determines If You Are Humble 33
10 Humility Determines If You Will Stumble 37
11 Humility Determines If You Are Teachable 41
12 Humility Determines If You Are Reachable 45

Key #4: Integrity
13 Integrity Requires Character 49
14 Integrity Requires Courage 53
15 Integrity Requires Commitment 57
16 Integrity Requires Congruency 61

Key #5: Energy
17 Energy Comes From Health 65
18 Energy Comes From Environment 69
19 Energy Comes From Relationships 73
20 Energy Comes From Passion 77

Key #6: Vision
21 Vision Inspires Hope For The Future 81

22	Vision Inspires A Strategy For Success	85
23	Vision Inspires A Plan for Priorities	89
24	Vision Inspires Your Daily Agenda	93

Key #7: Excellence

25	Excellence Means Taking Responsibility	97
26	Excellence Means Shining, Not Whining	101
27	Excellence Means Getting Results	105
28	Excellence Means Giving An Extra Inch	109

INTRODUCTION

We all have hopes, dreams, and goals that we want to ACHIEVE. From big dreams and life goals to New Year's Resolutions or even career goals, achievement in life is something we all strive for and must have in order to be successful. Unfortunately, how to be successful isn't something that is taught in school or college.

How to ACHIEVE in life wasn't something my parents taught me. How to find success, regardless of how I defined it, wasn't something addressed in the training for any job I've ever had. How to ACHIEVE goals in life was something I learned the hard way – by trying, failing, trying again, and succeeding – over and over again. I took many wrong turns along the way, and I certainly have regrets over poor and sometimes foolish decisions.

I've been blessed to have some wonderful people in my life who were able to help me learn some hard lessons. I've had role models who showed me what to do – and what not to do. Putting it all together requires one to consider how to be intentional about setting and achieving daily to-do lists, weekly goals, and life dreams.

What I'm defining is the essence of self-leadership. The tips on each key area contained in this book are critical to leading ourselves in order to accomplish things in life. It takes all of the factors I'm including. Intentionally applying them will enhance and accelerate your progress. No one ever wakes up and realizes they have accomplished significant things accidentally.

The letters in ACHIEVE stand for:

- Attitude

- Choices
- Humility
- Integrity
- Energy
- Vision
- Excellence

Achievement is not something we do. It is something we are. It is a state of being, not a state of doing. These principles will help you ACHIEVE, unlock your potential, become successful, and even become significant in the lives of others.

Knowledge alone is not enough. I'll be giving you some tips on how to ACHIEVE in your life, but they must be applied to have an impact. Reading them is only the first step. Whatever your goals and dreams are, you will have to work to get there. Investing time, energy, and even money into developing yourself will help you get move toward your goals.

Achievement and success require dedication and hard work in addition to the tips included in this book. It's also important to keep in mind we must continually work for achievement. If we ACHIEVE one goal and simply stop there, we are not truly living life. Standing still is not an option. Life moves on, regardless of our feelings about it. Time goes on, we can't change that. We simply must learn to move forward and to adjust.

Achievement is much like mountain climbing – no one gets there accidentally. Certainly no one ever accidently climbed to the top of Mount Everest. Consider some great achievers in history: Diana Nyad swam from Cuba to Florida with no shark cage – an amazing accomplishment that certainly didn't happen accidentally.

Thomas Edison did succeed in creating the light bulb – but only after thousands of attempts. Team Hoyt biked and ran across the U.S. in 45 days, and that was most certainly intentional.

I'll be giving you examples for each key area and sharing stories from my life where I have successfully applied the principles found in this book. And, I'll also be giving you examples of when I failed to apply the principles. We can learn more from our failures in life than our successes if we reflect on the lesson and apply it in the future.

Challenges and failures in life actually help us because they allow us to learn how to succeed and overcome obstacles. It is a fact that we will fall, and we will fail in life.

When we convert our failures into lessons, they become positive experiences and provide us with valuable insight on how to succeed in the future. We can choose to learn the lesson and benefit from it, although I know that can sometimes be difficult. However, it's much better to learn the lesson than to repeat the mistake.

What qualifies me to write this book is my track record of achievement in life to date. Not because I'm special. But, because the principles work when we apply them, and I've diligently applied them for many years. They worked for me; they will work for you.

I'm excited to share the lessons I've learned to help you create an achievement model for your life. Let's get started.

CHAPTER 1
ATTITUDE CREATES POSITIVITY

"What we believe determines how we behave."

~ Andy Stanley

I didn't get a head start in life.

My father sexually abused me from age 12 – 19, forced me to play the role of his wife, beat me, raped me, and even shared me with others.

I didn't know how to handle the pain, shame, and false sense of guilt from those years of abuse. Life was, at times, almost not worth living. I once considered ending it.

I met my husband Mack when I was 19. He was my knight in a shiny Camaro. He gave me the courage and support to escape, and I didn't look back.

I left behind the father who had abused me, and I left behind my mother who blamed me for it all. I left with a couple of pillow cases stuffed with my clothes and a determination that my past wasn't going to hold me back.

I didn't really know how to deal with what happened to me, so I did the best I could at the time. I locked seven years of my life up behind a closed door in my heart. And then, I threw away the key.

I realized I could spend the rest of my life playing the victim role and using what happened to me as an excuse not to enjoy the rest of my life. Or, I could survive, move on, and learn to thrive. I chose to thrive.

What happens to us in life isn't what's most important. What's most important is how we allow it to affect us. We don't always get to choose what happens in life. We do get to choose how it affects us and how we respond to it. We can choose our attitude about what happens.

Attitude creates positivity.

Attitude can make or break the situations you face every day. It's not easy, but making a decision to have a positive attitude and to be grateful for what you have can turn a bad situation into a good one.

My friend Amir Ghannad, author of *The Transformative Leader*, often talks about the power of our mindset in a situation. He says, *"Your view of what is going on is influenced far more by what you say to yourself about the situation than what you actually physically see or hear."*

I was working a side job as a waitress at a steakhouse many years ago. I had a full time job and was also taking night classes.

One Saturday night, I got a large table of 10 people in my section. The kitchen was running behind. When the party ordered appetizers, I rushed to place the order with the kitchen. Fast service meant a bigger tip, and I was working hard with a smile. In the back, the appetizers came across the hot food line. I loaded up my serving tray with a platter of golden fries covered with bacon and cheese and a bowl of ranch dressing on the side. With the addition of a stack of appetizer plates, the serving tray was full.

I lifted the tray to my shoulder and grabbed a stand for the tray on my way out the door. As I left the kitchen, I noticed one shoe felt loose. I decided to ignore it since my hands were full as I moved through the restaurant.

I almost made it.

Less than 10 feet from my table, the shoelace that had come untied found its way under my other shoe. As I firmly placed that foot down and lifted the other, the issue became clear. It's easy to have a good attitude when things are going my way. It was much more difficult to have a good attitude when I crashed to the floor in a pile of cheese fries, ranch dressing, and broken appetizer plates.

Right then and there, I had a choice.

That could become the worst waitressing moment of my life. Or, it could simply be a moment. It was about how I chose to take it. I got up and decided to disregard the ranch dressing dripping down my shirt! I decided to laugh about it, and smile, even though I was sure my table was going to be upset because those were clearly their cheese fries on the floor. But, they also had a good attitude and were very patient about getting their food. Our attitude about what happens is important. Our attitude towards other people is even more important.

John Maxwell said, *"85 percent of success in life is due to attitude."* Our attitude toward life will determine life's attitude towards us. The interesting thing about attitude is we get to choose it.

We can look at any situation in our lives and choose to see the positive or the negative side of things. As Marianne Williamson said, *"Joy is what happens to us when we allow ourselves to recognize how good things really are."*

It's truly up to us to focus on what we can control – our attitude. Stephen R. Covey calls it *"re-scripting"* ourselves into a proactive state where we choose our response to the situation. Start with being grateful for what you have, rather than bitter about what you don't have.

CHAPTER 2
ATTITUDE CREATES POSSIBILITY

"How we think shows through in how we act. Attitudes are mirrors of the mind. They reflect thinking."

~ David Joseph Schwartz

It's our perspective as a victim or victor that will determine our success in life. Bad things happen to everyone at some point. We don't choose to be victims in life. But, we can choose to be survivors. As Stephen R. Covey said, *"Victimism gives your future away."*

A positive mindset creates possibility for the future. A victim mindset causes us to give away what's possible in the future because if we aren't looking for the positive things in life, we won't find them.

Attitude creates possibility.

My first job was working as a server at a pizza restaurant. I worked the lunch shift, Monday through Friday every day, from 11 – 2. Most customers would have the all-you-can-eat pizza and salad buffet because it was fast and didn't cost too much.

I was the only lunch server for all 36 tables in the restaurant. My job was to set up the buffet, keep the salad bar stocked and clean, make the tea, fill the ice bin, stock the soda machine, answer the phone, take delivery orders, greet the customers when they entered, take and fill their drink orders, keep dirty plates bussed, refill their drinks, check them out at the cash register, clean the tables, chairs, and floor after the customers left, wash all the dishes, put them away, and restock everything before I left. All for $2.13 per hour, plus any tips I made.

The lunch buffet was $5.99, and a drink was $1.35. Most customer bills came to less than $8.00 for lunch. The average tip is 10% for a buffet, so the best tip I could expect would be about $1.00 – and that's if I hustled really hard to keep their beverage refilled and the dirty plates bussed. If I was too busy and the customer ran out of tea, I may not have gotten a tip at all.

I learned a lot of things during my years of waiting tables, off and on, earlier in my career. You see the best and the worst of people when you wait tables.

I learned quickly my attitude affected my tips. If I didn't smile at the customers, they thought I was unfriendly. If I didn't greet them enthusiastically, they didn't feel welcome or appreciated. If I didn't remember the names of the regular customers and what they liked to drink, they often wouldn't even leave me the change from their dollar.

Attitude is the one thing that changes everything. I don't mean your attitude on the days things are going right. I mean your attitude each and every day, even when things aren't going your way. Your attitude reveals all someone needs to know about your character. If you are positive, it will show. If you are negative, it will also show. Having a positive or negative attitude will impact your level of success.

Your attitude will affect both your feelings and your actions. John C. Maxwell said it this way, *"We are either the masters or the victims of our attitudes. It is a matter of personal choice."*

If you carry with you an attitude of positivity and hope, people will want to be around you. If you carry an attitude of negativity and complain, people will not want to be around you.

Motivational speaker and author Nick Vujicic said it best, *"Often people ask how I manage to be happy despite having no arms and no legs. The quick answer is that I have a choice. I can be angry about not having limbs, or I can be thankful that I have a purpose. I choose gratitude."*

Nick Vujicic was born without arms or legs and

suffered from bullying as he grew up. He often felt like a burden on his family. However, he is now a world renowned speaker, father, and evangelist. He hasn't let his physical state hold him back from creating a life where he impacts millions of people all around the world. He is one of the most positive people I've ever met. I've even seen videos of him surfing, swimming, and golfing!

He chose to be positive and his attitude of positivity has created possibility in his life.

Focus on what you can control. Focus on what you can do. Focus on what you can influence. When you focus on these things, they increase.

We are often very good at creating excuses as to why we can't do something. Even worse, we eventually talk ourselves into believing our excuses. Then, they become limiting beliefs.

Don't spend your life making excuses or creating reasons why you can't do something. As Thomas Jefferson said, *"Nothing can stop the man with the right mental attitude from achieving his goal; nothing on earth can help the man with the wrong mental attitude."*

Our attitude creates possibility and possibility creates hope. When we have hope, we experience a fundamental mindset shift and expect something good to happen instead of expecting something bad to happen.

That's why positive mental affirmations are so powerful. When you reflect on empowering thoughts about success rather than reasons for failure, you will find what you focus on expands. We literally create our future one choice at a time. The first and most important choice comes down to our attitude: our outlook on life.

CHAPTER 3
ATTITUDE CREATES PERSPECTIVE

"The habit of being happy enables one to be freed, or largely freed, from the domination of outward conditions."
~ Robert Louis Stevenson

Carey Lohrenz was the US Navy's first female F-14 Tomcat fighter pilot.[1] To say she faced challenges in her career is an understatement. As a female in a male dominated field, she had to break through more than a few barriers to be successful. Perhaps, the most challenging obstacle she faced was an obstacle she faced early in life. It's also likely the one that gave her the perspective to overcome all the other challenges she later faced. Carey was born without fully developed hip bones. In fact, when she was six weeks old, her parents were told she would never be able to walk and would probably be in a wheelchair her entire life.

She underwent major reconstructive surgery and spent the first two years of her life in a plaster body cast from the waist down, holding her hips and legs in a frog-like position to allow her bones to develop the right way.

After she grew out of the need for a cast, she had to wear a brace with a bar between two boots that locked her feet into a position pointed out nearly 180 degrees from one another to keep her hips stable. Everyone but her parents believed she would never be strong enough to learn to walk, but eventually she did. Step by step. Inch by inch. She not only learned to walk, but she also became so physically fit that she was able to serve in the military and fly an F-14.

Carey's experiences in those first few years of life gave her a unique perspective which allowed her to approach all of her future challenges with an attitude of *"just watch me!"* Obviously, her attitude toward life served her well throughout her military career.

Carey says, *"We hear all these little messages and negative labels from naysayers, starting at an early age: You're not smart enough. You're too slow. Too young. Too old. Too inexperienced...Too whatever. And, these discouragements don't always come from evil people who want to see us fail. Quite often, they come from people who love us and care about us...Sometimes they have good intentions; they don't want to see us hurt or disappointed when faced with a challenging reality. So, they try to lower our expectations."*

Carey learned to keep a good perspective when faced with challenges. That helped her maintain a positive attitude in the face of adversity, challenge, and danger.

Our perspective of challenges determines our response to them. When we view a challenge with a positive perspective, we see an opportunity. Even when we fail, the right perspective allows us to learn and to be more likely to succeed in the future.

Think of when a toddler learns to walk. He or she falls many times, eventually learning to walk by learning what NOT to do. And yet, we don't call it failing to learn to walk.

Failing only becomes failure when we quit trying.

The right perspective gives us the tenacity to keep trying again and again as we learn what NOT to do while we're also learning what we can do or should be doing.

Learning is based on having a growth-oriented mindset which allows us to realize failure, mistakes, and obstacles don't define us. The right attitude provides a perspective of *this situation will provide an opportunity for growth.* instead of *my lack of ability is going to limit my success in this situation.*

The right attitude provides a perspective of *my ability isn't predetermined but rather my effort and attitude determines my ability.*

Without an attempt, there will be no experience.

Carol Dweck, author of *Mindset: The New Psychology of Success*, believes success in any area of life is dramatically influenced by how we think. She writes, *"My research has shown that the view you adopt for yourself profoundly affects the way you lead your life. It can determine whether you become the person you want to be and whether you accomplish the things you value."*[2]

I mentioned how I started my career waiting tables for $2.13 an hour plus tips. There is nothing wrong with waiting tables, and I was proud to be earning my own money for the first time in my life. But, it didn't take long before I realized I didn't want to do that the rest of my life.

It would have been easy to use my lack of formal education as an excuse not to improve myself or my circumstances. It was daunting to realize I would need to spend *years* working while going to college to earn the degree that would qualify me for the job I wanted.

Because I was homeschooled, I had never been to any type of school. I didn't have a diploma. Starting from ground zero was tough. I started by taking my GED exam and passing it. Next, I enrolled in community college, took classes at night, and worked during the day. In all, I spent 10 years going to college while working full-time and often had part-time jobs too in order to graduate with my MBA. But, I did it. And, I did it with a cumulative 4.0 GPA. My perspective was *I can.* and *I will* instead of *it will take too long.*

Our attitude creates perspective. Perspective positions us for success or failure.

CHAPTER 4
ATTITUDE CREATES POTENTIAL

"Handicaps can only disable us if we let them. This is true not only of physical challenges, but of emotional and intellectual ones as well…real and lasting limitations are created in our minds, not our bodies."

~ Roger Crawford

I've shared how possibility thinking creates hope and how your perspective positions you for success. But, attitude can do more than that. Attitude creates the hope and potential of something better in the future.

How? Because it focuses our attention on the possible instead of the impossible. It shifts our thinking and our mindset from negative to positive, and the shift in mindset is what creates the potential for the future to be better.

Far too often, our situation feels worse than it is because we focus on the emotions and feelings in the moment rather than the fact of our ultimate freedom – the ability to choose our attitude in any given situation. It's not always an easy choice. In fact, most often, it's not an easy choice. But, you can look at anyone who has achieved anything great in history, and you'll find that person had a positive attitude. You can look for the opportunities or the obstacles. Either way, you will always find exactly what you're looking for.

We all face adversity, challenges, and obstacles in life. The key to success is learning to look beyond the challenge to see the potential in the future. We all have feelings of discouragement, disappointment, and frustration. But, we don't have to focus on them. Abraham Lincoln pointed out, *"Let no feeling of discouragement prey upon you. And in the end, you are sure to succeed."*

It really does come down to not letting negative attitudes prey on you. It's not always easy to do, and no one gets it right 100% of the time. But, the more we practice being positive, the more potential we release.

Be diligent in defending your mindset.

Here are three keys to unlocking a positive attitude:

Shift Your Thinking

When you feel a negative attitude of any kind creeping in, stop immediately and ask yourself why you are feeling that way. Identifying the *why* won't make the feelings go away, but it will help you consciously shift your thinking to something positive instead.

I like to use the analogy of a train station. There are two trains at the station. One will be traveling on the negative tracks. Destination: darkness, despair, and destruction of positive emotions. The other train will be traveling on the positive tracks. Destination: positivity, possibility, and potential. The train you choose to board will determine your emotional destination.

Motivational speaker Sean Stephenson suggested, *"The next time you find yourself stressing out, look for what's funny in the situation instead of what's 'not fair.' You're holding a very powerful flashlight: your conscious awareness. Be very careful where you shine it, because that is what you will choose to focus on."*

Shift Your Language

Our words are powerful because the words we speak determine the reality we seek. Our language, whether positive or negative, reveals our mindset. We should guard carefully the habits we create with our words.

Listen to yourself talk sometime. Are your words and phrases positive or negative? Some examples of negative language: *I have to. I hate to. I can't. It's not fair.*

Some positive language examples: *I choose to. I get to. I'm grateful for.*

Shift Your Behavior

Physical behavior helps create mental emotions. Have you ever gone to the gym even though you didn't really feel like it? Maybe you told yourself, *"Just go for 20 minutes,"* but you ended up feeling better and stayed 45 minutes instead. You behaved your way into an attitude change.

William Glasser said, *"If you want to change attitudes, start with a change in behavior. In other words, begin to act the part, as well as you can, of the person you would rather be, the person you most want to become. Gradually, the old, fearful person will fade away."*

How would a positive person act? What books would they read? What would they watch? What would they listen to? How would they spend their spare time? Who would they spend time with? What would they talk about? How would they start their day?

I know a lady who wanted to start her day more positively by exercising at 5:30 am twice a week. She isn't a morning person and doesn't like to get up very early. But, she does. Her secret? She sleeps in her workout clothes. *"I've figured out, if I put on my workout clothes before I go to bed, I'll feel like exercising as soon as I wake up,"* she told me.

Act like you like it, and you will begin to feel like you like it.

CHAPTER 5
CHOICES TODAY DEFINE
HOW YOU GO

"The history of free man is never written by chance but by choice — their choice."

~ Dwight D. Eisenhower

Our choices yesterday have defined our today. Our choices today will define our tomorrow. Success depends not on our circumstances, but on our choices. The choices we make today will determine our success tomorrow, next week, and even 10 years from now. Our choices determine where we go and when we go.

Big decisions like a career choice or whether or not to get married are important. It's easy to see how those choices will affect us. But, it's just as important to make the right little choices each and every day. Often, the little choices we make daily don't seem to make a difference.

That's the problem — it's often not a glamorous or important choice that defines us. It's usually those small daily decisions.

Little choices, like what books we read, how we spend our free time, or whom we spend our time with, don't seem like much in the moment. Add them up, and you will see how those little choices compound over time. We make hundreds or thousands of choices each day and can't always see how they will impact our future. But, they can be significant, even if we can't see it at the time.

Years ago, I decided I wanted to run a marathon. 26.2 miles sounded like a goal worth achieving, and I wanted that bumper sticker on my car! When I chose to sign up for the marathon, it was a big decision. Choosing to call myself a real runner was a defining moment. That choice didn't accomplish anything beyond costing me a $90.00 registration fee to get a bib number. I had to do something before I would accomplish something. I had to actually train to reach my goal.

It took months of training and dedication. Months of little choices every day about what to eat for lunch, how much water to drink, how far and how often to run, if I should cross-train, and if I should continue to teach my group fitness classes. I had to decide how to fit all that into my schedule while working two jobs and pursuing an MBA.

Those little decisions every day were much harder because it didn't really feel like they mattered at the time. However, all those positive choices added up over several months. I was able to finish the marathon and proudly claim my "26.2" T-shirt and bumper sticker. I bought five stickers because I wanted every car I bought in the future to have one too.

Our behavior is a product of our conscious choices based on our values. When we make decisions and choices based on our values, we know we are working towards success in our lives.

Eleanor Roosevelt said, *"I am who I am today because of the choices I made yesterday."* You are who you are today because of choices you made in the past. But, who you become tomorrow is based on the choices you make today. What you choose to spend your time, money, energy, and resources on demonstrates what is important to you. Choose wisely.

You can spend your time any way you want to, but you can only spend it once. Too often, we don't consider how valuable our time is. Our time is one of the things that should be most protected.

Anything or anyone that is not helping you move forward in the direction you want to go should be considered toxic. These things or people may not necessarily be bad, but they are still toxic to you and your future if they're not aligned with your values.

Eliminate the toxic influences from your life. End toxic relationships. Remove toxic temptations. Those are often difficult choices to make, but they determine the results you get in life. Bad choices lead to bad consequences. Good choices to good ones.

Our choices are determined by our values. If you value running a marathon, you are going to choose to spend your free time on Saturday morning running instead of sleeping in and having brunch. Once you have determined what you truly value, it's simply a matter of intentionally choosing how those values will be lived out in your daily life.

We often preach something like this to our children as we tell them who they should or shouldn't hang out with or who their friends should or shouldn't be. The friends your teenager is spending time with will influence, and sometimes determine, his/her future. If they are choosing to spend time with friends who are into drugs, odds are pretty good they will be influenced by that environment.

But, we don't always apply this principle in our own lives:

- What choices are you making related to spending time with your family?
- What choices are you making related to your health? Your eating? Your sleeping?
- What choices are you making related to your future?
- What choices are you making related to how you spend your spare time?
- What choices are you avoiding?
- What choices do you need to change? Why?

CHAPTER 6
CHOICES TODAY DEFINE HOW YOU GROW

"Wise choices in the beginning provide a better chance of success in the end."

~ Dee Ann Turner

Our choices determine how, and if, we will grow. Growth only happens when we are choosing to intentionally develop ourselves and to become comfortable with the discomfort of learning more and stretching ourselves to the next level and beyond.

Choices yesterday define today. We can't change decisions made in the past. We can't change the consequences of those decisions. We can only reflect on the outcome and learn from the mistake, so we don't repeat it. The growth opportunity comes from reflecting upon and learning from our mistakes. How do we choose to respond when we try something and aren't successful? Or, how do we choose to respond when we make a mistake? Will we grow through it and get better?

Years ago, I was responsible for the hiring decisions for the office where I worked. The front desk receptionist position was open. We needed someone immediately to answer phones, make appointments, and check-in patients.

Finding a qualified employee who required little or no training was always a challenge. The company used a staffing agency with a temp-to-hire model. The agency would send over candidates after screening them, and I would make the final decision. After I put in a request for the open front desk position, two candidate applications were sent over.

One didn't have the required computer skills, which left me with a young lady I will call Janet. I interviewed her. While Janet didn't have a strong resume with the required skills, she had some basic computer experience.

She seemed to be very easygoing and good-natured. I didn't carefully consider how her personality would fit with a fast paced front desk job.

She told me during the interview she desperately needed the job because her only other job offer was working night shift. She needed the daytime schedule to attend school at night. Deep down, I knew I should interview more applicants. I heard the phones ringing and ringing outside my office, while the other employees tried to answer them, cover the front desk, and do their jobs too.

I made a choice I would later regret. *"Okay Janet, you start tomorrow."* She accepted the offer, declined her other job offer, and showed up for work the very next day.

By the end of the week, I knew I had made a mistake. Janet had a great attitude. She was positive, willing to learn, smiling, and cheerful right up until 9:00 am when the office opened, and we turned on the phones. The problem was she couldn't handle the pressure of answering a non-stop ringing phone, checking-in patients, and getting the necessary paperwork completed accurately. She could do any of those things, but not at the same time or at the pace needed in a busy office.

Mistakes were costly in that environment. Failing to check-in a patient when they showed up meant the overlooked patient could sit for hours waiting for their name to be called. If their chart was never handed to the nurse, they wouldn't be called back. Worse still, making an appointment for the wrong patient meant the wrong chart was pulled, risking a mistaken identity mix-up.

Within three weeks, I knew I had to terminate her. Regretfully, I let her go. I was back in the same situation with no receptionist, ringing phones, and no one to check in patients. I had cost myself the time spent training an employee I had to terminate, and the expense of searching for, hiring, and selecting another candidate.

I had also wasted three weeks of Janet's time and potentially cost her other job opportunities.

Reflecting on poor choices can be difficult. No one wants to dwell on the lessons of the past, but they can be the best lessons. I learned to screen job applicants more carefully with consideration to the position. While Janet wasn't the last person I hired that wasn't the best fit, I did a much better job considering the application and applicant relative to the position that needed to be filled.

It's never easy to revisit our mistakes. But, how we choose to view those situations determines if we go through life or grow through life.

You first make your choices. Then, your choices make you. Our choices always come with consequences. While we can choose our actions, we can't choose the consequences that follow.

The consequences of the thoughts we think are the choices we make.

We should start by choosing our thoughts. Our thoughts determine our emotions. Our emotions determine our actions.

From that perspective, as Bruce Barton pointed out, *"Sometimes when I consider what tremendous consequences come from little things, I am tempted to think there are no little things."*

CHAPTER 7
CHOICES TODAY DEFINE
HOW YOU CAN GIVE

"When you decide to pursue greatness, you are taking responsibility for your life. This means you are choosing to accept the consequences of your actions, and to become the agent of your mental, physical, spiritual, and material success. You may not always be able to control what life puts in your path, but I believe you can always control who you are."

~ Les Brown

We all have the opportunity to make an impact and a difference right where we are.

I once thought you had to *"be somebody"* to make a difference. A celebrity, a famous person, or Mother Teresa.

But in truth, those who change the world start by changing themselves. They start by becoming a person who *can* influence others in a positive way. Then, they become a person who is *willing* to influence others in a positive way.

Improving ourselves equips us to improve others. However, accepting responsibility for your life and accepting responsibility for the lives of others requires sacrifice.

Our choices determine how we grow, but they also determine how we give and what we give.

I cannot give someone what I don't have to begin with.

Becoming more valuable so we can add value to others is a responsibility we shouldn't take lightly. As Stephen R. Covey said, *"To touch the soul of another human being is to walk on holy ground."*

That's why I read 50 personal growth and leadership books every year. I'm working on developing myself, so

I'm better equipped to help others. It's the best way I've found to equip myself to give to others.

We can choose to give to others in many different ways depending on our relationship with them, what their needs are, and what we have to offer.

Some people choose to give money. Some choose to give time. Others choose to give opportunity. There are endless ways to add value to others. Some people choose not to give. And, it's their loss. When you do something for someone they cannot do for themselves or when you give something to someone that they otherwise would not get, you gain far more than they do.

I like to give knowledge, insights, and experience allowing others to gain from the lessons I've learned over the years. That's one reason I write books – so I can pass along the nuggets of wisdom I've learned along my journey.

I also give time and encouragement. One way I do this is by teaching group fitness. It's not something I do because it pays well financially, but it pays dividends in so many other ways.

One of my most energetic and enthusiastic attendees is "Ms. Linda." She is 75 years old, and I honestly think she goes to the gym more than I do! While she has limitations on what she can do, she doesn't let that stop her. She goes to cycle class, aerobics class, and she walks on the treadmill. "Ms. Linda" and other people like her are why I love teaching group fitness – because when I can help make exercise fun and enjoyable, I can encourage someone to continue to invest in their physical health.

It's incredibly rewarding to help encourage someone to be intentional about their overall health and fitness. I've learned that when I can help empower someone's mind in one area, it will help empower them in other areas of their life too.

I make the choice to invest time developing my coaching skills and learning the choreography, so I can deliver a great fitness experience. However, if teaching group fitness begins to take too much time away from writing and speaking, there may be a point when it's no longer the best use of my time.

We all make choices on how we spend our time – and only we can decide if the return on investment (ROI) is worth it. Determining the ROI is different for everyone, but you will know you're on the right track when:

- You feel fulfilled while giving.
- You are passionate about giving.
- You aren't worried about getting paid for what you're doing.
- You look forward to opportunities to invest time giving.
- Giving doesn't leave you completely drained or exhausted mentally.
- The activity is something only you can do for someone.
- The activity helps you grow.
- The activity leverages your natural talents and abilities.
- You excel at the activity and are better at it than almost everyone else.

CHAPTER 8
CHOICES TODAY DEFINE HOW YOU WILL LIVE

"The price of greatness is responsibility."

~ Winston Churchill

Once we've determined what we truly value, then comes the hard part: Living out our values each day. That comes down to leading ourselves well. As my husband Mack says, *"If we can't lead ourselves well, we don't deserve to lead others at all."*

The key is saying yes to the right things and no to everything else. Remember, your choices today will determine your results tomorrow.

If spending time with your children is a priority for you, choose to schedule it into your week first. Will you work late or invest quality time with the children? Only you can decide which activity is most important.

You may very well have some activities you have said yes to in the past that are no longer in alignment with your core values as you become more intentional about selecting and living in alignment with those values. That's okay. As you become more aligned, it will be easier to re-evaluate opportunities as they arise.

Honor the commitments you have already made, but become very selective about the commitments you'll be making in the future. I very rarely say yes to anything on the spot anymore. I ask to get back with the person by the next day if possible. That way, I can consider the commitment carefully without feeling pressured, and it's much easier to say no with a gracious smile when I remember what else I could be doing with that time instead.

I am connected with thousands of people via social media and spend a large part of my day interacting with those people, posting motivational content for their benefit, and answering messages from them. One lady reached out to me recently. I'll call her "Jane." I've been connected with Jane for about a year, and we've talked on the phone but never met.

Jane enrolled in a personal growth program and part of the program is seeking out a mentor for regular and intentional mentorship sessions. I was honored she considered our interactions valuable enough that she reached out and asked me if I would be able to mentor her twice a month over the phone.

I asked for details and specifics about what would be involved and what the time commitment was. She told me we would have regular sessions twice a month via phone, for about a year.

I thanked her for considering me but shared with her my plate was full of activities I had chosen based on my values and long/short term goals. Overloading my plate would decrease the amount of time and reduce the quality of time I have available for my writing, speaking, fitness classes, clients, and other commitments.

To say no to something, we must have a bigger yes on our mind already. When we do, we are equipped to carefully weigh the cost of time involved and make an informed decision, rather than giving into the social pressure to say yes simply because someone asked. There likely may be a better person to take care of that task anyway.

If you want to maximize your potential, you must accept the responsibility for managing your time and energy well.

All of us are familiar with the concept of budgeting our money. Yet, we often fail to budget our time. And then, we wonder why it seems to have evaporated. Be intentional about identifying what's truly important to you. Then, say yes only to the things aligned with your vision and mission.

Fill your calendar, schedule, and your life based on *your* priorities. Then, say yes to *those* things. If your priority is to be a better parent, say yes to things that allow you to become a better mom or dad. If your priority is to become a better team leader, say yes to growth and development opportunities in that area. If you value becoming a leader in your church, say yes to opportunities that help you develop influence with church members.

What you say yes to defines your life.

If what you say yes to defines your life, what you say no to defines your legacy. You cannot do everything. Once you have determined what you will say yes to, learn to say no to everything else. Telling people no gracefully isn't easy. However, people will respect that you have priorities and aren't willing to compromise them. Saying yes to everything will derail your life.

Saying no creates the space to say yes.

I regularly evaluate my commitments and calendar and find it incredibly freeing when I need to remember why I want to say no sometimes. Spend some time reflecting on these three key questions:

- What activities are you currently doing that you want to stop doing? Why?

- What activities are you currently doing that you want to continue doing? Why?

- What activities are you NOT doing that you want/need to start doing? Why?

CHAPTER 9
HUMILITY DETERMINES IF YOU ARE HUMBLE

"No man has a chance to enjoy permanent success until he begins to look in a mirror for the real cause of all his mistakes."
~ Napoleon Hill

If you had the opportunity to meet any great person from the past who was highly effective, successful, and significant, you would find he or she was humble.

There are four parts to humility:
1) Realizing you aren't better than anyone else
2) Realizing you aren't perfect or mistake proof, and everyone else already knows it
3) Not taking yourself too seriously
4) Being willing to serve others

Humility is the fine line between confidence and arrogance. Confidence maximizes your potential. Arrogance destroys it. Confidence reveals character. Arrogance reveals insecurity. Confidence is knowing you can do something. Arrogance is boasting about your abilities. Arrogance is having too much pride and ego, which is a huge turn off for the people around you.

The first steps in overcoming too much pride are to realize it, acknowledge it, and then work to intentionally embrace humility as a bigger value in your life.

It's not that you don't realize your self-worth, but rather you don't focus on it. The problem isn't thinking *I have done well,* but rather thinking, *what a great person I am to have done it!* It's important to understand from your frame of reference the world appears to revolve around you. But for the rest of the world, it doesn't. Becoming more focused on other people and less focused on yourself will increase your influence with everyone you meet.

Humility is the foundation for maximizing your

potential. Humility helps you stay centered. Humility comes with maturity. Of course, maturity most often comes from learning lessons the hard way. However, we can also learn from the mistakes of others without repeating them ourselves.

To be clear, I'm not saying you shouldn't have pride in a job well done. If you worked hard, accomplished something, or reached a goal, you should have some satisfaction in having done so. Your brain is hardwired to reward you with endorphins when you accomplish a task which will help inspire you to set a new goal or target. But, guard against inflating your self-worth based on success.

Rick Warren advised, *"True humility is not thinking less of yourself; it's thinking of yourself less. Humility is thinking more of others. Humble people are so focused on serving others, they don't think of themselves."*

I worked for a large hospital several years ago. The first day of employment for every employee was spent in "New Employee Orientation" which was scheduled every two weeks. New hires had to wait to start their job until after they had attended the day long orientation at Human Resources. The first few hours were predictable – we learned where to park, how to turn in vacation requests, access HR policies, and what to do in the event of an emergency. We also had a session on the culture of the organization with a focus on customer service.

To my surprise, the CEO came in about mid-morning and handed out little "Payday" candy bars to all the new employees. He said he wanted to make sure we got our first "Payday." I was extremely surprised when he walked up, greeted me by name, and gave me my brand new employee badge. I was impressed he not only took the time to attend, but also learned the names of every new hire.

The next morning, I arrived early, so I could find my way around the hospital. I got to work about 7:15 and parked in the parking deck as I had been instructed the previous day. I was again surprised when I saw the CEO park his car in the deck a few spaces ahead of me and walk across the cross walk. Following a few hundred yards behind, I watched in amazement as he picked up the three newspapers laying on the ground outside the entrance.

Thinking someone had fallen down on the job of picking up the newspapers that morning, I mentioned it to my new supervisor.

"Oh no," she assured me, *"He does that every morning, and he delivers them to the outpatient waiting areas."*

"The CEO delivers the newspapers?" I wondered aloud.

"Yes," she replied, *"After all, what better way to remind everyone that the phrase 'It's not my job' isn't part of our culture? It's part of everyone's job description to take care of something they see that needs to be done."*

It was a lesson I never forgot. Regardless of our success, title, or position, we are never better than anyone else. We should never consider ourselves too good to take care of something when it needs to be done. Humility makes a far more memorable (and favorable) impression on others than arrogance because it communicates our intention to serve, rather than be served. We respect a humble person, we resent an arrogant one.

CHAPTER 10
HUMILITY DETERMINES IF YOU WILL STUMBLE

"You've got to be humble, so you don't stumble."
                    ~ Burl Cain, Angola Prison Warden

I remember hearing Warden Cain speak the words quoted above on humility soon after I first met him. He was sharing how he effectively transformed Angola prison from one of the worst in the country to one of the best. And, how he also transformed during the process.

Prisons aren't nice places to begin with, and Angola had the reputation of being one of the worst when Warden Cain took over. He admits to a lack of humility in the beginning, but he had a major perspective change after he was required to carry out an execution. He realized he wasn't going to be effective if he treated the prisoners as though he and the guards were better or above those whom they were charged with guarding.

He attributed the success of the turnaround to one thing, *"You've got to be humble, so you don't stumble"* he stated.

There was a fundamental shift in his attitude, and it affected the entire culture in an incredibly positive way, transforming and improving the interactions between guards and prisoners.

Humility gives us the ability to learn from mistakes. There are humble people who learn from their mistakes, and they bounce back. There are also prideful people who are unwilling to learn and therefore repeat the same mistakes.

Pride can cause you to place the blame on someone else. Those people who are prideful are insecure and isolated because they think everything is about them.

In 2007, I was working in a doctor's office when the office manager was terminated. I was interviewed for the position, and I felt I deserved the position.

Humility wasn't something I had much of at that time. I thought I was capable of doing a better job than anyone else. I had stepped up to a leadership role in the interim.

Pretty much everyone in the office thought I would get the position, and it appeared I would get the promotion. But, I had a fundamental problem - I was too proud. I wanted to control everything that went on. I wanted everything to come through me because I thought I was the only one who could and should make decisions in the office.

One morning, we were getting ready to open the office, and one of the older ladies who worked there sat down with me. What she told me changed my life. She said, *"Ria, you are very capable. But, everyone is concerned because you want to control us. You act like you know everything – you don't. We don't feel like you care about us."*

She was taking a risk by sharing that with me – I was her new boss. She didn't say it specifically, but she was telling me I didn't have humility. I knew in my heart, she was right. Looking back, I am not proud of how I acted in those days. I am proud of how I responded to what she said. Rather than continue to demonstrate too much ego and pride, I listened to what came out of her heart.

It was a defining moment for me. Instead of getting mad, I actually listened to what she said. It took time, but I changed my behavior and my feelings. More importantly, I learned I didn't know everything after all. In fact, the more I learned, the more I realized I didn't know.

I knew I had truly learned my lesson when I was able to tell her *"Thank you"* and how much her words made a difference in my life. We don't always know the impact we have on others. It was important to me to be able to tell her how she positively impacted my life. I'm glad I got the opportunity to do so. There have been other people in my life that impacted me as well. I didn't always take the time to tell them, but I should have.

You may have heard *"Pride goes before a fall."* We all make mistakes. If you aren't making mistakes, you aren't doing much. Being able to learn from those mistakes is a sign of maturity. No one expects you to be perfect and never make mistakes. We don't get in trouble for making the mistake nearly as often as we get in trouble for trying to hide it. Sooner or later, it will be discovered.

The best thing to do when you make a mistake is own it and take action to correct it. In the words of Thomas Merton, *"Pride makes us artificial and humility makes us real."*

Those around you already know you aren't perfect. What they want to know is, *do you know it?* Admitting mistakes and acting to correct them will build trust and increase your influence. Trying to cover them up will create distrust and decrease your influence.

Guard against having pride by remembering your limitations and weaknesses. Recognize what you can and cannot do, should and should not do, will and will not do. No one is great at everything. If something is not in your strength zone, ask for help rather than causing an issue because you are too proud to seek assistance.

Author C. S. Lewis said this about pride: *"There is no fault which makes a man more unpopular and no fault which we are more unconscious of in ourselves. And, the more we have it ourselves, the more we dislike it in others."*

CHAPTER 11
HUMILITY DETERMINES IF YOU ARE TEACHABLE

"It's what we learn after we know it all that counts."
~ John Wooden

Many years ago, I was traveling to New York for a business trip. My traveling partner for the trip was a director whom I reported to at work. I'll call her "Nancy." As a way to develop me, she informed me before we left that she would leave all travel details to me. Decisions on how and when to travel, driving, directions, hotel, and expenses for the trip would all be my responsibility.

The trip went smoothly for the most part. I learned some things about planning ahead, including a tip about how you should eat before checking out of your hotel to avoid dragging your luggage all over Times Square in search of breakfast. We ate breakfast the last day of our trip in McDonald's near Times Square with our suitcases resting under our feet. Nancy was true to her promise and didn't complain or question my decision to check out before breakfast.

I was pretty confident about traveling in general, and this certainly wasn't my first trip. But, there was some added pressure in trying to impress my boss. Traveling is always exciting, but there is some stress in trying to keep up with everything when you are away from home and away from your routine.

As our airplane landed on the ground at the airport in Atlanta, Georgia, only the final leg of our trip remained – the car ride back to Alabama. I breathed a sigh of relief internally. Nothing had gone wrong the entire trip. Our bags didn't get lost, we didn't get lost, and I was mentally congratulating myself on a job well done.

It was late September and hot. I was working up a sweat while wrestling our luggage into the trunk of my tiny car. Nancy wasn't physically as strong and was much older, so I tried to spare her from lifting our heavy suitcases.

With two suitcases, two carry-on bags, one laptop, and two purses, we had been well prepared for any emergency on the trip and experienced none. Wishing for more trunk space, I finally fit all the pieces inside and gratefully slammed the trunk. I was looking forward to the air conditioned ride during the 90 minute drive home.

As I walked around to the side of the car, I realized I had a major problem. I didn't have any car keys. Thoughtlessly, I had set my purse and keys inside the trunk while loading the suitcases. I frantically tried to open the car door, hoping I had unlocked it before setting my keys down.

I hadn't.

Mortified, I had to admit to Nancy I had locked my keys inside. There was a pause as she stared at me. Then, we both started laughing uncontrollably. Thankfully, I had my phone in my pocket. Within an hour, the locksmith was able to get us on our way again.

Anytime we are faced with having to admit a mistake, we should face it immediately, accept the responsibility, and then act to correct it. The sooner we do this, the quicker we can move forward.

In my case, I also accepted responsibility for the $60 charge from the locksmith.

Interestingly on the drive home, Nancy told me she would not tell anyone else in the office about the incident. If I wanted to share it, that was fine, but she would not make a joke about it to anyone. She let me know she was going to keep the story to herself. To this day, I don't have an issue telling the story and admitting my thoughtlessness, but I always have appreciated her sensitivity.

To be teachable means we're open to being taught. This definition implies being teachable is different than simply learning on your own. We are teachable only when we are open to learning from others.

Being teachable also means we don't take ourselves too seriously. Life expands when we realize perfection isn't attainable, and we are going to make mistakes. When we realize this, it gives us permission to try, "fail," and try again. We embrace the concept of trying something, making a mistake, and learning from it. In this case, we're not failing – we're learning, and that's a critical part of success and maximizing your potential.

You must be willing to try something new, stretch yourself outside your comfort zone, and reach for something potentially outside your grasp. But, how would you know if you never tried? Just think how ridiculous it would be if we had been afraid of making mistakes when we learned to talk? Learn to laugh at yourself, loosen up, and don't be afraid to make mistakes. As G. K. Chesterton said, *"How much larger your life would be if your self could become smaller in it."*

We are teachable when we ask for, listen to, and accept constructive feedback from others. Even when we don't ask for feedback, we should listen to and accept it.

When you make a mistake, start by accepting responsibility right away by admitting you made a mistake. Then, you can right the wrong.

CHAPTER 12
HUMILITY DETERMINES IF YOU ARE REACHABLE

"Humility is the true key to success. Successful people lose their way at times. They often embrace and overindulge from the fruits of success. Humility halts this arrogance and self-indulging trap. Humble people share the credit and the wealth."

~ Rick Pitino

Going the second mile isn't second rate. It's first class. Most of us already know when we put others first, we get far more than they do. As Douglas Lawson said, *"We exist temporarily through what we take, but we live forever through what we give."*

Servant leadership is a term coined in the 1970's by Robert Greenleaf. However, the concept of serving others has been around since the beginning of influence. A great example: Jesus, King of kings, washed the feet of His disciples.

Some people struggle with the concept of being selfless in their willingness to serve others. They expect everyone else to serve them. Serving others isn't about being their servant. It's simply about helping and being service-based. It's about serving others while leading others. Don't hesitate to reach out, be the first to help, help remove roadblocks, and help someone overcome an obstacle. Serving is helping.

A humble person realizes they should be open to interacting personally with others. Rick Warren said it best, *"You can impress people from a distance, but you must get close to influence them."*

Being humble is just as much about being reachable, approachable, and serving others as it is about being willing to learn.

I didn't do this very well for many years because I lacked confidence in myself. I had an attitude of *please go away and don't talk to me*, instead of *how can I help you?*

As I've developed more self-confidence, I've worked

hard to become more reachable.

There are two basic kinds of confidence: self-confidence and situational-confidence.

Self-confidence is conviction of your values and core beliefs enhanced by experience and lessons learned from both successes and failures. In other words, self-confidence is static. The factors that make you uniquely you create your self-confidence. Self-confidence is developed over time. While other people can support you, self-confidence will only be realized by growing and developing your own character.

Situational-confidence is certainty in the outcome of a situation which is enhanced by your knowledge, skills, and abilities. In other words, situational-confidence is dynamic and is affected by factors outside of your control. Situational-confidence can be increased by developing your competency.

You won't always have situational-confidence. There will be times when you try something new, take on a new job, or first become a manager and lack experience or technical knowledge. There will be times when you have a new relationship with a team member and lack confidence in their ability to get the job done.

You may have self-confidence because it's based on your character which remains the same in every situation but lack situational-confidence. For example, you may lack situational-confidence, perhaps in a new job, and still have plenty of self-confidence in your ability to learn.

That shows strength of character because it takes self-confidence to develop situational-confidence. The more self-confidence you have (when balanced with an equal amount of humility), the greater success and influence you will have.

When you are humble and approachable, others will realize it. They will be more likely to come to you for advice, you will have more influence with them, and you'll have better relationships with others.

Being reachable also means you aren't afraid to get your hands dirty, and you won't ask anyone to do something you aren't willing to do or haven't done.

I was working as an office manager in a physician office many years ago when a patient fell in our parking lot. He didn't realize how badly he was hurt. He also didn't want to tell anyone, so he went into the lobby bathroom and tried to clean himself up.

His scrapes were worse than he thought. He wasn't able to stop the bleeding with paper towels. To make things worse, he was on a blood thinner and ended up getting blood on everything in the bathroom: walls, counter, sink, and floor. He finally stopped the bleeding and ended up being okay.

But, the bathroom was a mess. Another patient discovered what happened and told us the bathroom needed attention. Word travels fast in a small office, so a team member quickly came and told me what happened.

I was working in clinic that day assisting one of the physicians, and I knew I had two choices: ask someone to go clean up the mess or ask someone to cover for me while I cleaned it up.

I donned some gloves and cleaned the bathroom myself.

William Arthur Ward said, *"We must be silent before we can listen. We must listen before we can learn. We must learn before we can prepare. We must prepare before we can serve. We must serve before we can lead."*

CHAPTER 13
INTEGRITY REQUIRES CHARACTER

"Character is the ability to meet the demands of reality."
~ Henry Cloud

Integrity has four components: 1) Character; 2) Courage; 3) Commitment (to self); and 4) Congruency (with others).

Character is the foundational component because all the other components are built on top of character. In fact, integrity is determined by character. And, character is the determining success factor in life.

Your character and integrity determine how you will face life's challenges. Your response to success, failure, joy, pain, sickness, health, poverty, wealth, and the *"demands of reality"* will all be based upon your character.

Character is based upon intangible characteristics that will determine your success: attitude, work ethic, perseverance, resilience, discipline, courage, humility, and many more. Character is not based upon, or determined by, your education, background, race, ancestors, or experiences in life. Each and every day, you are writing your internal script by choosing your values. Then, your script (resulting character based upon the values you have internalized) will dictate your decisions and responses in any given situation.

Competency is your talent, natural gifts, skills, and abilities. Our character, not our competency, determines how far we will go and what we will ACHIEVE. Unfortunately, many people spend years developing their competency and little time developing their character and integrity.

In June 2013, I went to Guatemala on a mission trip. This wasn't a mission trip like you usually hear about where you take medical supplies and teach the Gospel. It was a mission trip to start the cultural transformation of

Guatemala. This initiative had been years in the making because the President of Guatemala had asked John Maxwell for support in teaching the nation personal leadership principles.

While I was in Guatemala, our team trained various leaders; from Boy Scout troop leaders to top-level government officials. 150 coaches trained over 20,000 leaders in three days. One of the things we shared with them was 87% of who we are is determined by our character. The other 13% is what we know, our skills, knowledge and technical abilities. In other words, 87% of our success and influence comes from what we are, not what we know.

It's not always easy to live true to your values. Sometimes, having character requires you to face uncomfortable truths and stand up for what you believe. This happened to me early in my career.

I had recently been promoted to a new position in the organization where I worked. My new role was one of two identical positions in the organization. "Christy" (name changed) was my counterpart, and we had the same job duties and expectations. Christy had been there many years and had settled comfortably into her routine, so I knew I could learn from her.

I had a good work ethic, and I was eager to continue to make a good impression, hoping to continue moving up in the organization. Always a quick learner, I watched carefully how Christy did her job, and then I tried to see if I could make the process more efficient. I made some mistakes but quickly learned how to be more effective and efficient in my new role. And, I didn't mind working hard, taking initiative, and stepping up without being asked.

One day, my boss called me aside. *"Hey Ria,"* she said, *"Come here a moment."*

"Sure," I replied, *"What do you need?"*

"I've got a little problem," she chuckled, *"And, I need your help."* Always eager to help, I nodded for her to continue. *"Ok, sure."*

"Everyone has noticed how quick you are learning, and you are really doing an outstanding job."

"Thank you!" I smiled, excited she had noticed my efforts and hard work.

"But the problem is, you are making Christy look bad. She's been here a lot longer and you are causing some problems for her. There are some concerns about why she doesn't do as good a job as you are doing. And, people are asking me why I let her get away with slacking off."

I could feel my smile starting to melt. *"Oh?"*

"Can you just slow down sometimes and try not to be so fast at your work? I don't mean you have to screw up on purpose but maybe wait until someone asks you before you do something that needs to be done."

I couldn't believe it. My boss was telling me I needed to slack off because Christy didn't want to work hard.

I knew she and Christy were friends outside of work. They took trips together, went out for lunch, and even had drinks after work sometimes too. I also knew I wasn't going to slow down for one minute. I wasn't making Christy look bad, she was making me look good.

It put me in an uncomfortable position, but I told my boss I wasn't going to compromise my work ethic. And then, I showed her by continuing to work as hard as I could. Within two years, I had her job.

Character is having the right values. Integrity is living true to them. We must have the character to meet the demands of reality and the integrity to choose to do so.

CHAPTER 14
INTEGRITY REQUIRES COURAGE

"Real integrity is doing the right thing, knowing that nobody's going to know whether you did it or not."

~ Oprah Winfrey

Dr. Henry Cloud defines character as *"The ability to meet the demands of reality,"* and integrity as, *"The courage to meet the demands of reality."*

Courage is the second component of integrity.

The word *courage* comes from the Latin root word *cor*, which means *heart*. When we say courage, we literally mean, *be sincerely true to the heart.*

Integrity requires courage because it's not always easy to stand up for your values and for what's right even when we are afraid.

Nelson Mandela said *"I learned that courage was not the absence of fear, but the triumph over it. The brave man is not he who does not feel afraid, but he who conquers that fear."*

Having courage often comes with a personal cost.

It takes courage to stand up for something but even more so when it comes with a personal cost.

A soccer team of boys 11-17 years old, along with their coach, went exploring in Tham Luang cave after a scrimmage in the summer of 2018. Unexpected flooding due to a monsoon trapped them underground in the cave. Although they were reported missing within a few hours, it took over a week to locate them underground.

When they were finally located, rescuers realized the challenge of getting the team out safely was going to be almost insurmountable.

The flooding had cut off the boys' exit route and forced them deeper into the cave. They remained there for over two weeks while an international rescue team tried desperately to get them out. While the rescue team was able to get food to them initially, the depleting oxygen levels in the cave were reaching critical levels.

An international team of divers worked to get supplies to the boys and their coach while planning a rescue attempt.

Former Thai Navy Seal, Saman Kunan, was one of the divers who volunteered to try the risky maneuver of taking oxygen tanks into the cave. An avid athlete and experienced diver, he was highly trained. Although no longer in the navy, he participated in the rescue attempt.

Understanding the mission was very dangerous, he chose to go into the cave to deliver the much needed oxygen tanks. The trip into the cave and back out again took as long as 15 hours. Knowing it was the right thing to do, he wasn't focused on the potential personal cost.

For Saman Kunan, the personal cost ended up being extremely high. He delivered the oxygen tanks but didn't have enough in his own tank to make it back out of the cave. He lost consciousness in the cave and died.

Thanks in part to his efforts and sacrifice along with the efforts of nearly 1,000 others, the boys and their coach were all successfully rescued several days later.

Heroes like Saman Kunan inspire us. It's easy to think of this type of hero as having courage.

But, each one of us must have courage to face life with integrity based on the character we build within ourselves.

Andy Stanley writes about this in his book, *Like a Rock: Becoming a Person of Character*.[1] He shares his realization that although he listed honesty as one of his values early in his adult life, he wasn't always honest. He states, *"I found it easy to tell little, convenient lies if they served my purposes. After all, why sacrifice my reputation or risk losing a friend when a small 'fact adjustment' would easily smooth things over? I knew it was wrong...But, after I clarified my core values, a little lie was no longer a little lie. It was evidence of failure at the deepest level. It was a red flag signaling me that I was moving in a dangerous direction."*

Having enough integrity to share the truth, even when a little white lie might be more convenient takes courage. It takes courage to resign from a good paying job when you realize the company isn't ethical. It takes courage to learn something new and get outside of your comfort zone. It takes courage to admit your character flaws and intentionally work to improve them.

These situations challenge us to be true to our values. It takes courage to build character, just as entering a cave to rescue a soccer team takes courage. You can have courage without integrity, but you can't have integrity without courage.

As Billy Graham once stated, *"Courage is contagious. When a brave man takes a stand, the spines of others are often stiffened."*

Our reputation comes from other people and what they believe about what they see on the outside. Having character and integrity means focusing on improving what's on the inside. If you focus on the inside, as time passes, you will also become better on the outside. Abraham Lincoln is famous for saying, *"Character is like a tree and reputation like a shadow. The shadow is what we think of it; the tree is the real thing."*

True integrity is having the courage to do the right thing even when no one is watching. Integrity is not only about what happens in public with others, but also about what happens in private within ourselves.

CHAPTER 15
INTEGRITY REQUIRES COMMITMENT

"Unless commitment is made, there are only promises and hopes…but no plans."
~ Peter Drucker

We often think about integrity as telling the truth, being honest, or not stealing. Those with integrity will exhibit all of those things which are very good character traits. But, integrity also includes keeping the commitments made to oneself.

The statistics on how many people make New Year's Resolutions only to fall through on them are rather ridiculous. We get excited by the concept of a fresh start and make a promise to ourselves we aren't 100% committed to keeping. If we were completely committed, we wouldn't be breaking our resolutions. A research study by Statistic Brain Institute[1] showed only 9% of people felt they were successful in achieving their resolutions. In fact, 42% of people never succeed and fail to keep their resolutions *every year.* [1]

We know why we want to change in the first place, but seldom do we have enough integrity to keep the commitments we make to ourselves. That's because we are externally motivated, instead of internally inspired.

Motivation is external, but it doesn't last. Inspiration comes from within, and it does last.

Those who are motivated from the outside aren't bought in to why they should change their behavior in order to reach their goal. In other words, their values, or what they truly care most about, have not changed. Therefore, their behavior change is short lived.

We must be internally inspired and completely committed when we make a commitment to ourselves. That means, mind and body are in alignment with what we think and what we do. We know why we want to change, and we have the strength of character to keep that *why* firmly in sight.

When you set a goal or task for yourself and successfully reach it, you are building a successful track record which will help you create momentum for something bigger. When you set and keep commitments to yourself, you are also building your personal integrity account. Anytime you make a commitment to yourself but don't keep it, you are destroying your personal credibility with yourself and making it less likely that you will keep future commitments.

You want to build credibility by setting small, easy to achieve, goals to start with. Then, build up over time. You may not be able to commit with integrity to losing 10 pounds this month because you have tried before and failed. But maybe, you can commit with integrity to eating a salad today instead of a burger and fries.

Setting a goal is always the easiest part of achieving it. Quite frankly, commitment is a lot of work. It's not any fun. It's difficult and sometimes even painful. However, it shapes our character and makes us who we are.

Commitment to yourself often means following through when you don't feel like it. Sir Edmund Hillary said, *"It is not the mountains we conquer, but ourselves."*

Take action now. Don't wait until you feel motivated to act; act until you are inspired to keep going. Don't wait or put off doing something because the longer you wait, the more difficult it will become to actually do it. If you need to have a difficult conversation with an employee – do it now. If you've been putting off a chore around the house, take care of it now instead of waiting until later to do it. Commitment takes discipline.

Discipline is a *mind muscle*. Just like your physical muscles, the more you exercise it, the stronger it becomes. Mark Twain suggested, *"Do something every day that you don't want to do. This is the golden rule for acquiring the habit of doing your duty without pain."*

We probably all have a tendency to procrastinate on doing something we aren't excited about. It's easy to push it to the bottom of our to-do list when we don't want to do it, and there's no definite deadline for getting it done. If that's the case, give yourself a definite deadline and make it public. Make sure it's reasonable of course. Research has shown we are much more likely to accomplish goals when they are reasonable, measurable, and dated.

One thing I've learned about discipline is if there is something I don't want to do, it's very easy to find excuses not to do it. So, I deliberately minimize or eliminate distractions to make it easier for myself. I turn off notifications on my phone at times because I need to focus on writing a chapter or a blog. It's all too easy to see an email pop up which, if read, can easily lead to checking LinkedIn messages, Facebook notifications, Twitter hits, etc. Before I know it, 20 minutes have disappeared from my life, and all I've really done is avoided doing what I needed to be doing.

If you want more discipline in one area of your life, it can help to create more discipline in other areas of your life. Much like starting small creates momentum, so does achieving other goals. This is why I set a physical goal each year, such as running a marathon. I'm intentionally creating more discipline in my physical life which will help me be more disciplined in other areas of my life. Success in one area is likely to create momentum in other areas.

CHAPTER 16
INTEGRITY REQUIRES CONGRUENCY

"Promises are only as strong as the person who gives them."
~ Stephen Richards

Commitment is about keeping the promises you make to yourself. Congruency is about keeping the commitments you make to others, both verbal and implied.

Congruency can be defined as *"in agreement"* and it means we walk the talk, do as we say we will, and practice what we preach. What we say and what we do are in alignment, and others can depend on that.

Verbal commitments are the promises we make to others. Implied commitments are those we make when we state our values to others. Implied commitments are broken when we claim to be someone we aren't.

If someone tells others he or she values people but treats the server at a restaurant like an object instead of a real person, he or she is breaking an implied commitment. They didn't actually make a promise to us to treat the server at the restaurant nicely, but they implied it when stating how much they value others. How we treat those who can do little or nothing for us reveals our true character.

Why is congruency important? Human relationships work – or don't work – because of trust.

We build trust or create distrust with every interaction with others. Every time we interact with someone, we are making deposits into or withdrawals from the emotional trust accounts of others. Although we seldom make accidental deposits, we often make accidental withdrawals.

Making deposits requires us to be intentional each time we interact with someone. The goal should always be to build trust and integrity. Integrity is the one thing we all value and expect in every relationship.

The American Management Association sponsored a study of more than 1,400 managers from around the United States. 225 values and traits were assessed, and one very important question was asked of those who were surveyed, *"What values, personal traits, or characteristics do you look for and admire in your superiors?"* The number one response was, *"Integrity, is truthful, is trustworthy, has character, has convictions."*

That's not surprising. If you ask ANYONE what they most want in relationships, I believe it will be integrity and consistency between what someone says and does.

When we're congruent, we don't pretend to agree with others when we don't. For example, I have several friends who are vegan. I respect that. If I go to their home, I take a dish that is vegan, respecting their food values. However, I don't practice a vegan lifestyle in my own home nor do I pretend to be vegan while I'm in their home. There is a difference between respecting the values of others and pretending to share them.

Are you the same person everywhere you go?

If you have a high degree of character, integrity, and congruency, you are the same. For example, you don't have to worry about being one person at church and another person outside of church. If you say one thing and do something different, you will quickly lose trust with others. In relationships, the little things are the big things.

As Ralph Waldo Emerson stated beautifully, *"What lies behind us and what lies before us are tiny matters compared to what lies within us."*

Congruency isn't just about walking the talk, it's also about keeping your word. Do you keep the tiny commitments you make? If you can't be trusted to keep the small commitments, you won't be trusted to keep the big ones.

We don't always think about the many ways we can unintentionally break our commitments. Have you ever told someone you would meet them at a specific time, but you were late? For some reason, you broke the commitment you made. Perhaps, it was due to something out of your control. A traffic accident may have delayed you. Or, you simply failed to plan appropriately. If it happens repeatedly, others come to realize they can't trust you to do what you say you will do.

That's why we should carefully consider the commitments we make. It's much better to say *no* than to give a *yes* you can't honor. Making a commitment we can't or don't intend to keep means we not only break trust with the other person - we also break trust within ourselves.

Teaching group fitness has long been a hobby of mine, and I've had the privilege of teaching at many gyms over the years. When we moved to Atlanta, I had to resign from the gym I had taught at for seven years. On my last day, one of the members said, *"Ria, you have never missed a class without letting us know you were not going to be there. And, you always got someone to teach in your place. I could always count on you."*

That was one of the best compliments I ever received because I felt it revealed one of my core values: keeping commitments.

The member was right. I never missed showing up for a class without getting a substitute. One time, I even taught with the flu because I had committed to be there and couldn't find a substitute.

CHAPTER 17
ENERGY COMES FROM HEALTH

"The pain of discipline weighs ounces. Regret weighs tons."
~ Jim Rohn

Your mind is your most precious resource. You use your mind to create, dream, think, reflect, plan, organize, read, write, study, learn, and grow. Your brain is a physical organ that allows you to consciously think, make decisions, and choose responses.

Your mind (your thoughts) direct the brain, which controls the rest of your body. Research shows thoughts, whether positive or negative, actually create physiological changes in the brain.

This allows us to accomplish tasks in the physical world. The body fuels the brain and provides it with access to the surrounding environment through the senses. In other words, our brain is dependent on the eyes to see, the ears to hear, etc. The brain processes the stimulus in our environment, but the mind controls our response, with the exception of automatic reflexes of course.

The healthier you are, the more energy you will have. Your health will determine how much energy is available to your brain and body. How are you fueling and treating your brain and body? You should be intentional about caring for your body relative to food choices and exercise, along with rest and rejuvenation. Proper self-care and good health are critical to maximizing your potential.

My point is to be intentional about creating positive health habits to maximize the creative potential within your mind. Positive health habits can be broken down into a few different areas. However, I'll focus on the top two: eating and exercising. Other things certainly affect your health, such as stress or mindset, but I'll focus on those in other chapters.

Eat For Health

Food serves as fuel for the body. What you eat, how you eat, and when you eat impacts your brain, body, and mind. Eating too much processed junk food causes your body to store the excess calories and sugar as fat. Eating too little causes your body to switch into conservation mode. Eating a balanced diet consisting of mostly whole, healthy foods provides your body with the appropriate vitamins and minerals to properly fuel yourself.

It amazes me how many people *aren't* concerned with the ingredients in the food they eat. Many years ago, Mack and I did a nutritional reset where we fasted from some food groups, including sugar, for an entire month. I had to learn to become very intentional about reading the ingredients on everything we consumed for a whole month. It was incredibly shocking to discover how much sugar is in processed foods. Because of what we learned during the process, our pantry and our diet look completely different today. While we still indulge at times, we have learned how healthy eating impacts our energy. If you eat bad foods, don't be surprised if you feel bad.

Food can also serve as an emotional crutch or social activity, and we must be intentional about managing that as well.

For the most part, we should consider what we eat as fuel and make healthy choices about what we are putting into our body. Become intentional about what you are eating and become knowledgeable about how it affects your mind and body. Then, if you want to make a choice to indulge, you'll know when and how often you should.

When it comes to food, be informed and intentional about what you are doing and why you are doing it.

Exercise For Health

Exercise creates endorphins, the body's natural, positive chemical response to the right amount of exercise. Exercise doesn't have to be done at a gym. Go outside and take a walk, hike in the woods, swim, walk while you are talking on the phone, or do some stretching. It's much easier if you enjoy it.

Tom (name changed) went for an annual checkup and while he was there, he mentioned to his doctor that he was having trouble with balance and low blood pressure. His doctor gave him some balance exercises to do and told him not to worry about the blood pressure since he was an avid runner. Tom worked on the balance exercises but was still having trouble when he went back the following year. It was several more months before he was referred to a specialist where they discovered Tom had lost over 30% of his hearing on the left side.

Concerned, the specialist ordered some scans and sent Tom home to await the results. Tom and his wife, Judy were out celebrating their 36th wedding anniversary when the specialist called and told Tom he had a brain tumor the size of a golf ball.

Surgery would be very difficult due to the location of the tumor, so Tom opted for 30 radiation treatments instead.

Although now inactive, the tumor is still present. Tom suffered some side effects both from the tumor and the radiation. But, he didn't let it stop him from running nearly every day *even during treatment.* Tom ran a half marathon just days after finishing his last radiation treatment and continues to run regularly, even to this day.

Exercise puts life's problems into perspective.

CHAPTER 18
ENERGY COMES FROM ENVIRONMENT

"When a workplace becomes toxic, its poison spreads beyond its walls and into the lives of its workers and their families."
~ Gary Chapman

I was once working in a job where there was a three way tug of war going on between the office manager, the physicians who saw patients in the clinic, and the corporate leaders who managed the entire organization. Everyone wanted to blame everyone else for anything and everything that went wrong. It was, at best, a toxic environment and you could have cut the tension in the office with a knife.

Stress levels soared, morale plummeted, and you never knew which policy to follow on which day of the week because you weren't sure who was winning at the moment: the physicians, the office manager, and the corporate leaders all had competing agendas.

When stress goes up, morale goes down. The energy in your environment influences how you feel. Odds are, you've also experienced a situation with tension or negative energy in your workplace. How did it affect you?

Your environment must be aligned with your values before it can have a positive impact on you. Environment isn't only related to where you work. Environment at home matters too. Does your home environment make you feel better or worse?

When I was growing up, the environment in my home was always a mess. On the rare occasions when we were expecting company, my mom would rush around frantically at the last minute, picking up clutter and cleaning madly. Today, a clean house without a lot of clutter is very important to me. When the house is a mess, cluttered, or dirty, I don't feel good. Our environment influences how we feel and how productive we are.

I find it nearly impossible to be highly productive when things around me are a mess. If you drop in, you might find a few things out of place. But overall, I keep my environment in an orderly state. I'd never be ashamed if someone dropped by. It's much more peaceful that way. Anytime I get stressed out, you will find me cleaning, organizing, and sorting.

Maintaining my environment helps me have more positive energy. The last thing I do before leaving for a trip is make sure everything is organized and clean because I don't want to return home to a messy house.

I have a morning ritual to straighten up or clean up something every day. Even the little things make a difference. Put the dishes in the dishwasher instead of leaving them in the sink. I straighten the pillows on the couch. Fold the laundry right away instead of leaving it in the dryer to fold later.

Because order is something I value, I want it reflected in my work space too. I want my desk organized, so I can find things quickly. The first thing I do when we move is start unpacking and organizing my desk. I can't really work until everything is back in place.

I have systems in place to keep up with things, so I don't spend precious time searching for something lost. I read an interesting statistic that claimed Americans spend more than two days a year searching for lost items.

Whether you value structure and order like I do or you value creative clutter, what's most important is that your environment suits you and supports you.

In 2014, I resigned from my job to pursue writing and speaking full time. About a month before my last day at work, I started cleaning out the spare bedroom in our house for my new home office. It was time to get serious.

In previous years, I didn't need an office although I had many projects that required me to write, think, and create. I had started college in 2002 and continued nearly non-stop until I graduated with my MBA in 2012. Two of my degrees were accelerated executive programs, which meant lots of online coursework outside of the classroom and papers to write.

I had also written grant applications for the non-profit mountain biking organization Mack and I helped organize in 2011. We were awarded over $100,000 for the grants, which required quite a lot of time researching and writing.

Until 2014, I had always worked (when I worked from home), studied, and done my writing either at the dining room or kitchen table. In the summer, it was quite pleasant to do homework from the kitchen table overlooking the pool in the backyard. However, it was also distracting.

I knew when I started writing and speaking full-time, I needed a dedicated, organized environment in our home that would support me in those goals. I needed a place where I wouldn't have to pick up my papers and books every time we had a meal or someone stopped by.

What does your environment say about you? What does it tell others about what you value? If I spent time in your environment, would I find positive books to read, thought-provoking videos to learn from, or a beautiful space to think and create? Do you have a dedicated place for thinking, reading, writing, and reflecting? You may not have it right now, but you can certainly work toward having it in the future.

Your environment is not only related to your house, car, or office. It also relates to the relationships in your life.

CHAPTER 19
ENERGY COMES FROM RELATIONSHIPS

"Look carefully at the closest associations in our life, for that is the direction you are heading."
~ Kevin Eikenberry

There is no doubt the relationships and connections in your life can be positive or negative, but the type and quality of relationships in your life are determined by your values, thoughts, and actions. For some, this will be a difficult pill to swallow.

At times, you may not accept responsibility for your life because it's easier to blame external conditions instead of internal ones. Once you realize your internal conditions affect your external circumstances, you must accept the responsibility for making improvements if you're not 100% satisfied with your life. Since you're reading this personal growth book, you're most likely not satisfied with where you are. That's a sign you are ready for growth.

There are two ways in which we can increase our energy relative to our relationships: 1) Develop character ethic; and 2) Intentionally develop high quality relationships and social connections. Since we covered character ethic in chapter 13, let's look at developing relationships that will give you energy.

Just as we must say *no* to some opportunities in life in order to say *yes* to others, we must be intentional about saying no to some relationships before we'll be positioned to develop the right relationships. When we're committed to growth, we must leave some people behind.

It doesn't mean we don't love them, but it does mean we no longer share the values the relationship was based on. For example, you tell your teenager to stop being friends with one of their peers who starts making bad choices. *"They are a bad influence on you,"* you might lecture, *"Don't continue to hang out with them."*

It's easy when it's someone else. It's more difficult to do in your own life. But, the principle is the same. The wrong relationships will always influence you in a negative way. The right relationships will always influence you in a positive way.

Your character will determine the relationships you value. Your commitment to intentionally adopt the right values will help nurture those relationships.

Who you are determines who you spend your time with. As Jim Rohn says, *"You become the average of the five people you spend the most time with."*

Who are the five people in your life that you choose to spend the most time with? Not necessarily your co-workers, although they can influence you, but you may or may not be choosing to spend discretionary time with them.

Write down the names of the five you spend the most time with by choice. These people influence you the most.

Now ask yourself: How would you describe their lives? Are they positive? Are they committed to personal growth? How do they spend their spare time? How do you feel when you're with them? Do you make better or worse choices when you're with them?

How are each of these people helping you get to the next level? Do they help you grow in some way? Or, do they hold you back? Do they encourage you? Or, do they discourage you? Are they keeping you average? Or, are they helping you become exceptional?

It's not that we are better than anyone. None of us are better than anyone else. But, our relationships influence our energy, positively or negatively, and ultimately determine our level of success.

Evaluate the five on your list. Do you want to continue spending time with each of them? Should you? If not, what type of person would you want to spend time with instead? You don't have to stop caring about them, but you may need to travel in a different direction.

If the people you have close relationships with aren't helping you achieve your goals or supporting your journey, the relationship is not helping you grow.

Those who are satisfied with average want you to be average. They will continue choosing to spend their time on activities that don't increase their value or take them forward in life. Your desire to grow will confuse them.

You should end all toxic relationships. People who are intentionally holding you back should no longer have a place in your life. This may be a hard choice, but to maximize your potential, you must become intentional about getting those with negative energy out of your life.

After I left home at 19, my mom visited me a few times. Every time she came, she told me I was going to Hell for my decision to leave my family, including my abusive father, without their blessing. I quickly realized I didn't need that toxic relationship in my life if I was going to move forward. I told her not to come back unless she could be supportive of me. It doesn't mean I don't love her, but it does mean the relationship wasn't positive. I needed to end it, and I did.

We've all left people behind in order to continue moving ahead to better relationships. You may miss them, but you can love them without spending time with them. The *"unfollow"* button works beautifully for negative people in the virtual, social media environment. Remember, you can *"unfollow"* people in real life too.

CHAPTER 20
ENERGY COMES FROM PASSION

"Be fearless in the pursuit of what sets your soul on fire."
~ Jennifer Lee

You cannot achieve something extraordinary without passion. Passion is the spark that will ignite your soul and fuel you long beyond the point where you would have otherwise quit.

Passion is what separates someone who is achieving greatness and excellence from someone who is just doing a good job. When you are passionate about reaching a goal, you will not hesitate to sacrifice things of lesser value in order to achieve it. Those who are truly passionate about something and living their purpose know nearly everything is of lesser value.

You can't buy passion. It's priceless.

When we are passionate, we are inspired to work harder, dream bigger, and realize more of our potential.

Passion is literally defined as a compelling or strong emotion. It's derived from the Latin word *Passus* which means to suffer or submit. In Theology, it means Christ's willingness to suffer on the cross and die for us.

When we are passionate about something, we are willing to suffer for it.

In the words of Kevin Hall, *"Suffering isn't necessarily a bad thing. It can and should be a good thing. It's noble. It's sacred. It's life defining. It's one thing to suffer and be a victim; it's an entirely different thing to be willing to suffer for a cause and become a victor…When we discover what we are willing to pay a price for, we discover our life's mission and purpose."*

If your passion is to be a stay at home parent and your spouse supports that passion, it will be easy to be the best parent in the world for your children. You won't mind sacrificing sleep to stay up with a sick child. You won't mind baking cookies for the cheer squad or making endless trips to little league practice.

If your passion is to build your own company, it will be easy to put your life savings into starting the business. You won't mind staying up until midnight to work on the business plan or learning to design your own website. You won't care that you spend your spare time networking and building your business instead of hanging out with friends.

You shouldn't have trouble identifying what you are passionate about. Whatever excites you, makes you happy, makes you smile, gives you energy, and whatever you enjoy doing so much you would pay to do it is what you are passionate about.

Some people discover and harness their passion at a very young age; others take many years, if ever.

Your passion and life's work should be aligned with your purpose.

Passion is what sent Mother Teresa to minister to the poor, sick, and dying in India. She discovered her calling and was willing to suffer personal hardships because she was passionate about it. She was in alignment with her purpose.

You can be passionate about something that isn't in alignment with your purpose. That's a hobby, not a calling. Make sure you clearly differentiate your hobbies from your purpose.

Passion Produces Energy

When you are passionate, you will work much longer and harder than if you aren't excited about what you're doing. That's why entrepreneurs often don't mind working seven days a week. They enjoy what they're doing and don't consider it work. Confucius said, *"If you love what you do, you will never work another day in your life."*

Passion Inspires Others

Ken Hemphill said, *"Vision does not ignite growth, passion does. Passion fuels vision, and vision is the focus of the power of passion."* Passion is contagious. It's exciting. It attracts others to you. When other people feel your passion for your vision, they will get behind you and help you turn it into reality. Far too many people settle in life. Those who don't settle for average, routine, or comfortable have fire, enthusiasm, and joy in their daily lives. They inspire many others to follow. They give us hope that life doesn't have to be dull or boring. As Nelson Mandela said, *"There is no passion to be found in playing small - in settling for a life that is less than the one you are capable of living."*

Passion Unleashes Potential

According to Jean De La Fontaine, *"Man is so made that whenever anything fires his soul, impossibilities vanish."* When you are passionate about what you're doing, you are far more likely to be successful because you will be more determined. There are many roadblocks on the road to success. You must be determined in order to navigate them as you unleash your potential.

Passion enables you to say *no* to the good, so you can say *yes* to the great. Passionate leaders don't settle for mediocre, simple, standard, or easy. As Norman Vincent Peale said, (they) *"...shoot for the moon and, even if they miss, land among the stars."*

CHAPTER 21
VISION INSPIRES HOPE FOR THE FUTURE

"The future belongs to those who believe in the beauty of their dreams."

~ Eleanor Roosevelt

If you don't have the vision of what is possible for the future, you won't be willing to work toward it.

Have you ever spent time actually considering what you want your life to look like in the future? Most of us go through life by accident. We graduate school, find a job, meet someone, grow older, and talk about *"the good old days"* when we get together with friends. When we stop to actually consider the direction we want to go, we create a personal vision and activate our subconscious compass to help guide us there.

Years ago, something I read challenged me to create my personal vision. I spent time reflecting on what I wanted my life to look like. If I could create the life I wanted, the life of my dreams, what would I create? I even wrote it down and then typed it into a note on my phone. Interestingly, almost every single item I envisioned has become my reality. What's also interesting is since I created that vision, I've grown. And, so has my vision. I now have a bigger vision for the future, and I'm continually working toward it, consciously and subconsciously.

There are four components to creating and implementing your personal vision: 1) Hope for the future; 2) A strategy for success; 3) Identifying and planning your priorities based on your values; and 4) Execution of action items in your daily agenda.

You may have heard, *"Hope is not a strategy."* But, you need hope, or you won't create the strategy for success.

What is hope? Where do we get it from? What if we don't have any?

Hope is an attitude of the mind that says, *"It's possible."* Researcher and author Brené Brown stated, *"Hope isn't an emotion; it's a way of thinking."*

It's the way we think about the future. Ludwig von Mises said humans require three things before they will act:

- *Dissatisfaction* with the present state of affairs
- A vision of a *possible* improved future state
- *Belief* that we can reach that future state

Many people have *dissatisfaction* with the present. That's not unusual. Few people truly realize they have the power to actually create their future, and even fewer are prepared to take action.

We get hope from the *belief* that we can actually achieve the future state we desire. *It is possible.*

If we don't have hope, sometimes it's necessary to borrow it from someone else. That's another reason why the relationships in our lives are so important. We need to have someone who believes in us when we don't believe in ourselves.

When I was 17 – 18, I didn't have a lot of hope. In fact, there were times I considered ending my life because I didn't have any hope the future would be better than the present. My friend Helen taught me a lot about hope.

Helen was originally from England, and she was the librarian at the tiny library in the community where I lived. We had a shared love of reading and although she was much older, we struck up a friendship. I was always in the library browsing the shelves for new books to read. Helen got me interested in learning to play bridge, which turned out to be a great outlet. I was allowed to join the local bridge club. It was considered safe by my father because there weren't any potential boyfriends involved, because the club was filled with retired seniors.

Helen introduced me to Wanda, who eventually became my regular bridge partner. The two of them were friends and included me in many of their activities. I realize now they were trying to take care of me even though they had no idea how desperate my situation really was.

Unfortunately, Helen was diagnosed with pancreatic cancer far too late to do anything about it. I knew she was dying, and it was so hard to watch her waste away over the summer. Her daughter Claire came from England to stay and take care of her during those months. I enjoyed getting to know Claire as well.

I went to visit Helen one day, and Claire was sitting with us. We all laughed about the difficulties of getting a *"decent"* cup of tea in the hospital, but I was ready to cry. I could see she was getting very weak, and I said something about *"there not being much hope."*

"There is always hope," Helen replied, *"And, I'm going to be a grandmother!"* She patted her daughter's hand.

Shocked, I looked at Claire. How could they celebrate that a baby was going to be born when Helen wasn't going to be around for the birth?

Hope is about *how* we think. We can always find something positive to hold on to. Helen passed away a few weeks later, but she forever changed the way I looked at my own situation. If she could have hope about the future even as she was dying, I could have hope about my future too. Hope begins with vision. Hope comes from believing what we want is within our reach. It's possible, as long as we are willing to continuously reach for it and *willing to let go of what's holding us back.*

CHAPTER 22
VISION INSPIRES A STRATEGY FOR SUCCESS

"Create the highest grandest vision possible for your life because you become what you believe."

~ Oprah Winfrey

Find your vision before deciding your strategy.

You may not know yet where you want to go, but you should have a good idea of where you don't want to go. Start there, and the next step will come.

In 2012, I graduated with my Master's in Business. For several years, I had a goal of getting an MBA. I had worked and gone to school for so long it was just a way of life. I worked all day and studied almost every night. My goal was to graduate and be done with college, so I could have a life. Because I had that goal, I gave up a lot of fun things over the years. I spent so much of my time working toward that goal. When I reached it, I just stopped. I stopped because I had reached the goal. I didn't have a vision for where I wanted to go next in life.

I remember a conversation I had with my boss at work soon after graduation. I respected her greatly, and we were talking about my progress at work. It was a *what's next* conversation about me. I asked her opinion and she smiled.

"Have you thought about Law School?" She suggested. *"Law school? ME?"* I had just completed more than 10 years of sacrificing most of my free time to earn my MBA. I felt like I was out of jail, and I wasn't about to go back! I hadn't formally developed a vision for my future, but I did know law school wouldn't be a part of it.

If we are sure which direction we don't want to go but not yet sure where we do want to go, we can start to narrow our focus by taking small steps forward on the path of personal growth.

Once you develop a clear vision, you need a strategy to

get you there. But, vision comes first.

Michael Hyatt tells us, *"If you have a clear vision, you will eventually attract the right strategy. If you don't have a clear vision, no strategy will save you."* That is very true.

It's like driving down the road where there are thousands of signs that have helpful information. If you don't know where you are going, the signs won't help you get there.

In my book, *PRIME Time: The Power of Effective Planning*,[1] I shared some exercises that will help you clarify your vision based on your personal definition of success. Whether your vision is to grow in your career or lose 10 pounds, a strategy will help you get there. You'll need a strategy because converting your vision into a better future requires a change in behavior, something that's incredibly easy to say and incredibly difficult to actually do.

All the strategic thinking in the world wasn't going to help me until my vision was clear because I didn't know where I wanted to go. Once I clarified my vision for the future, I figured out the strategy I needed.

Strategy is a high level plan. It's the overview of the map of your life and requires you to know where you are and where you want to go. Your strategy becomes a map that will guide you there.

Although strategy doesn't have to be complicated, we often make it complex. I've seen extremely complicated strategic plans for organizations that required complex spreadsheets, quarterly reports, and detailed metrics. That's not necessarily a bad thing, but it can cause the team to lose sight of the vision.

Strategy should serve the vision and become a tool to help you achieve it, not a burden that creates more work.

Strategy creates focus, which allows you to filter out

the other, less important, items. When it comes to strategy, focus on less, so you can achieve more.

In *The 4 Disciplines of Execution*,[2] authors McChesney, Covey, and Huling teach that success hinges on four disciplines. The first, is to focus on the *"wildly important goal."*

In other words, strategy starts with focus.

The best strategy tool I've ever seen or heard of is one simple question you can ask yourself once you know where you are and where you want to go. When presented with an opportunity, before taking action, ask yourself, *"Is what I'm about to do going to move me in the right direction?"*

If the answer is yes, then take action.

If the answer is no, then don't.

As an executive, team member, CEO, or entrepreneur, this simple strategy is incredibly powerful. As a human being, this simple strategy is life changing. Because, so often we waste time, money, and energy on the wrong things. We often waste precious resources on things that don't matter and then wonder why our vision for the future seems to move farther way. When that happens, your vision is not moving in the wrong direction. You are.

Statistics show you are up to 300% more likely to be successful when you are very specific about your strategy.

Strategy creates clarity. If you know where you're going, you can get there because clarity of vision creates clarity of purpose and priorities.

CHAPTER 23
VISION INSPIRES A PLAN FOR PRIORITIES

"Your schedule should not be based on what you need to do, but rather what you want to become."

~ Bill Hybels

I always thought I knew what my priorities in life were, until something I read challenged me to consider a new perspective. Now I realize, telling others my priorities is meaningless. What matters is how I live.

My priorities show up in my life. I don't have to tell people what is important to me. They can simply look at how I am living and see what my priorities are.

There are three ways to identify what is important to us.

1) What we spend time on:

We can spend time any way we want to, but we can only spend it once. Time is the most precious thing we have. You can't turn back time, save time, buy time, or manage time, but you can *waste* time. We are all given the same 1,440 minutes in a day. How we choose to spend our time is entirely up to us. How we choose to spend our time will determine where we will be in the future and what we will be doing.

For example, I invest some of my time working out almost every day because I want to be healthy enough in two months, two years, or two decades to enjoy life. If I believe my body is a temple, I need to take care of it. After all, it's the only one I'm ever going to have.

2) What we spend money on:

If someone took a look at my bank statement for the past month, they would know EXACTLY what is important to me: Books! Each month, I choose to spend discretionary funds on books I can read to develop myself. I invest my money in resources that will help me grow and develop in the direction I want to go. I spent more on books and personal growth last year than I did on clothes.

3) What we think and talk about:

James Allen said, *"A man's mind may be likened to a garden, which may be intelligently cultivated or allowed to run wild; but whether cultivated or neglected, it must, and will, bring forth. If no useful seeds are put into it, then an abundance of useless weed seeds will fall therein, and will continue to produce their kind."*

What we think about becomes our reality because we talk about what we think about, and then, those words lead to our actions. It's important we are thinking the right thoughts and talking about things that are meaningful to us.

So often, we are so busy for every single minute of our day that we don't accomplish the really *important* things. It's easy to spend all of our time and energy on activities that don't necessarily help us achieve the things we want to achieve.

We often talk about prioritizing our schedule, but what's most important is scheduling our priorities.

With your planner or calendar in front of you, stop for a moment to visualize this exercise. Imagine you have a large box in front of you that represents all 168 hours in the week ahead. The box has a lid that fits on top, and the lid must fit properly – nothing can spill out over the edges or overflow the top.

Every single thing you need and want to do this week must fit into the box. You will only have time for what you're able to fit in the box.

Think about how we typically plan our week. We start by throwing the *easy* things in first, because they are easy. After the *easy* things are in the box, we usually toss in the things we *must do*. Work, pick up the children from school, grocery shopping, pay the bills, etc.

After the *easy* things and the *must do* things are in the box, there isn't much room left for anything else. The box is full, and we close the lid on it with a sigh. Who has room for the gym? *"Maybe it'll fit next week,"* we tell ourselves.

Notice what happened – we put the lesser important items in first. Then suddenly, the box was full. There wasn't much time for important activities like enough sleep, personal growth, etc.

If we pack the most important priorities into our week the box first, we will find the smaller stuff somehow squeezes in the cracks and gaps, but now we've made time for our priorities.

Only you can decide what is a priority based on your vision, and only you can plan your life so those priorities come first.

CHAPTER 24
VISION INSPIRES YOUR DAILY AGENDA

"The secret of our success is found in our daily agenda."
> ~ Tag Short

This is my favorite part about vision – execution. Thomas Edison is attributed with saying, *"Vision without execution is hallucination."*

You must have both vision and execution to be very effective and successful. Highly successful people separate themselves from everyone else by implementing and executing a strategy that will create their vision.

I'm a *"doer."* I like to make things happen, tick the boxes, and check things off my list. In fact, I sometimes complete a task that isn't on my list and must write it down simply for the satisfaction of checking it off. There is incredible satisfaction in accomplishing something. And, the more difficult the task, the more satisfaction in accomplishing it. The trick is to not become overwhelmed and to break the task down into small, manageable steps.

Success is the result of taking disciplined and consistent action forward every day. Forward progress compounds over time. We cannot *"build Rome in a day."* Nor can we create, build, or achieve any other significant dream, vision, or goal in a day. But perhaps, we can in six, 12, or 60 months.

John Maxwell wrote about disciplined execution in his book, *No Limits: Blow the Cap off Your Capacity*.[1] Maxwell believes success is based on the *"rule of five."*

He explained, *"Let's say you want to cut down an enormous tree in your yard. How would you approach the task? I suggest you use the rule of five. Every day, go out to the tree with your ax and take five cuts. That's it? You may be thinking. Yes, that's it. Here's why it works. If you take those five cuts every day, week after week, month after month, year after year, the tree will fall."*

You won't always feel like it. In fact, you might not often feel like it. Success happens when you don't feel like it, but you do it anyway. What goes into your daily agenda determines where you are tomorrow and 10 years from now.

Maybe your goal is to write a book. You don't have to write the entire book in one day. You can write one page a day or even one paragraph. And one day, it will be finished. Maybe you want to lose 10 pounds. You can't lose 10 pounds in a day (short of cutting off your leg), but you can cut a hundred calories from every meal. If you do that long enough, (assuming everything else is equal) you will lose weight over time.

Success in your daily agenda comes down to discipline. It's the ability and willingness to sacrifice something now for what you want in the future. Discipline is giving yourself a command to act on the commitment, and then following through on it.

Discipline can be leveraged when it is timely, value-based, and consistent.

- Timely – Tomorrow's success is based on today's discipline.

- Value Based – Your actions each day should be based on your vision.

- Consistent – Consistent discipline over time leads to transformation.

As Pablo Picasso said, *"Action is the foundational key to all success."*

Take the time to identify your *"rule of five."* Or, the five things you need to do consistently every day to eventually chop down the tree, write the book, earn that degree, get to the next level, or start a business. Then, every day, you consistently execute those five priorities. You don't have to do them all day, just do them every day.

"What about on weekends?" You may be thinking. Yes, do them on weekends too. *"What about holidays?"* You wonder. Yes, do them on holidays too. Every day. Every day that ends in "Y." Every day.

Then, as you look at your daily agenda every morning, ask yourself one question:

What is the most important thing that MUST get done today? The one thing that if it doesn't get done, nothing else matters?

And, then do it. There isn't any secret to this. Of course, it's easier to say than it is to do.

I keep a little electronic sticky note on my computer desktop with the most important things I need to do. There may be several things on it, but I only focus on the most important one. Once that's done, I can move on to the next one. Having several allows me some flexibility. If I hit a roadblock on the most important one such as waiting on something before I can finish it, I've already got the next one there, so I don't have to wonder what I should be doing while I wait.

Your ability to implement priorities in your daily agenda will allow you to carry out your strategic plan and implement your vision. As Henry Ford said, *"You can't build a reputation on what you are going to do."*

CHAPTER 25
EXCELLENCE MEANS TAKING RESPONSIBILITY

"We are what we repeatedly do. Excellence, then, is not an act, but a habit."

~ Aristotle

Don't EVER settle for average when you can do better. What we do becomes who we are. If we settle for mediocre in anything, it becomes a habit.

When it comes to excellence, we must take responsibility to give more than is required. Excellence is far above and beyond average. And, average is relative. Wherever you are standing at the moment is average. Average is relative compared to what you are capable of, and none of us are living up to our potential.

To be excellent in something, we must take responsibility for giving more, doing more, and being more. Not because we are competing with others but because we are competing to be better than the person we were yesterday.

Only exceptional people are committed to excellence. Most people are comfortable with just getting by. And, that's perfectly okay if these people are happy in life. But, what you will often discover is most people want life to be different, but they aren't willing to put the work in to change it – starting with working on themselves.

Years ago, I was a new employee when my manager gave me a project. She asked me to create an Excel spreadsheet for our department projects. She sent me the assignment via email. I rushed through it, throwing together a quick spreadsheet without even formatting it. I sent it back to her within an hour. I thought she would be impressed because I accomplished it so quickly.

Within minutes, she sent me a response; *"This is a good start – now work on making it look professional."* Professional? Hmmmm. I had to think about that. I knew how to format in Excel. At the time, I thought that was not the point of a spreadsheet, and it would take too long to make it neat and professional looking. Bosses want speed more than anything – or so I thought. I worked on it a little more, added a few things like some colored fields and borders around my tables, and sent it back to her early in the afternoon. Satisfied with myself, I went to lunch.

When I got back from lunch, I had another email from her. *"Let's talk."* Uh-oh. That probably wasn't the *"job well done talk"* I was hoping for.

Later on that afternoon, she asked me to stay and talk after the rest of our team had left. I had no idea what was wrong, but I knew something wasn't going my way. She handed me a print out of the Excel spreadsheet and asked me what it looked like to me. I had no idea what the right answer was.

Slowly and with kindness, she showed me the typos and the misspelled words I had completely overlooked in my rush to get the project done. She talked about how important it was to make sure my work reflected the quality that I wanted it to.

I will never forget what she said, *"Once you put your name on something like this, it's done. For years and years to come, someone will be looking at this, and it will have your name on it. What they see will determine what they think about you and your work ethic."*

Wow! That hit me like a truck. I had never really thought about how important it was to BE EXCELLENT. I had never realized my work was a reflection of my character. Poor quality *when I was capable of more* meant I simply didn't care to do better.

It was a lesson I have never forgotten. When we do something, big or small, how we do it tells the world how excellent we are or are not. When you take something on and agree to do it, make sure you do it to the best of your ability. As Ben Carson said, *"It's not what you know but the kind of job you do that makes a difference."*

That's why it's so important to focus and work in your strength zone (relative to competency, skills, and abilities). You can only become excellent in an area where you are naturally gifted. At best, you will only be average in an area where you are not.

Excellence means doing more than you have to, and it means doing so on days when you don't feel like doing it. A commitment to excellence is exactly that: a commitment made by you.

It may seem difficult, and it is. There are days you won't feel like giving your best. There will be days you consider just getting by and settling for *good enough*. However, it's easy to be exceptional when you are fully committed to excellence and others are not.

Consider the experience eating at a Chick-fil-A® restaurant. Almost without fail, the experience is always positive at Chick-fil-A®. Why? Years ago, founder Truett Cathy decided average wasn't a high enough standard. He didn't want a restaurant that was just good enough, he set a standard of excellence. Years after his death, the experience at Chick-fil-A® continues to raise the bar for the fast food industry. They're not perfect by any means, but striving for excellence sets them apart. They go above and beyond by doing more than they have to do in order to sell chicken sandwiches.

Choose to build your reputation on a commitment of personal and professional excellence because it demonstrates a high level of character.

CHAPTER 26
EXCELLENCE MEANS SHINING, NOT WHINING

"You must be ready when your opportunity comes. You don't get a second chance to seize a once in a lifetime opportunity."
~ John C. Maxwell

The word excellent comes from the Latin root word *excellēns* which means first-rate, superior, admirable, or worthy. The quality will be higher and the value greater.

Those who are determined to ACHIEVE are willing to work for excellence and give their best. They realize a commitment to excellence makes them more valuable in so many ways because it's easy to stand out when you aren't willing to settle for average.

When you have a commitment to excellence, you prepare for opportunities before they arrive. The work must be done inside you to develop your character. Then, when opportunities come, you'll be positioned to seize them. As a result, you'll be shining instead of whining.

When opportunities present themselves, they often look like challenges to those who are unprepared. Someone committed to excellence won't see a challenge, but rather an opportunity. An opportunity to shine rather than whine.

I started teaching group fitness many years ago because I enjoy it, and it helps me stay in shape. About six months after I first started teaching, the manager who hired me resigned. A new manager was hired almost immediately. But, this new manager had different ways of doing things: New policies, new schedules, new everything.

I didn't like it. I didn't want things to change, and I wanted everyone to know it. I wanted the new manager to handle everything just like the one before.

Looking back, I'm not proud of my attitude at the time. I could have done so much more to embrace the change and make the new manager feel welcome. Instead, I let my frustrations about the changes be known. I didn't shine. Instead of stepping up and staying committed to excellence, I chose to whine to anyone who would listen.

It took a while before I realized I was the one with the problem. It was even longer before I realized I had missed a valuable opportunity to grow my influence and build a relationship with the new manager.

Instead of focusing on moving forward, I dug in my heels and held myself back. I got exactly what I deserved. The new manager knew I wasn't willing to be flexible. As a result, I was the last person to know about any upcoming or proposed changes. There wasn't any need to seek my feedback or ask for my input on making things better at the gym because I was resistant to any and all changes. I wasn't committed to excellence if it meant changing, which meant I wasn't committed.

I did eventually learn my lesson. When it comes to excellence, those who whine will be left behind by those who shine. Excellence means responding proactively to the situation and focusing on what you can improve, rather than what you can't.

Commitment to excellence affects your relationship with yourself as well as your relationships with others.

When you have a reputation of excellence, you have more influence with more people because they know they can trust you at a higher level.

For example, if you are considering a different healthcare provider, you probably either ask your acquaintances for recommendations or you search online to see what kind of reputation the doctor has before you make an appointment. You want someone who has a commitment to excellence when it comes to your healthcare because it means you can trust them to do more than be average. And, we all want excellence when we're on the receiving end of the relationship. The challenge is to have the same commitment to excellence when we're providing the product or service.

When you set a high standard of excellence, you raise the bar for yourself and those around you. Raising the bar increases your influence. People are attracted to and follow those who are exceptional. No one gets excited about mediocre people getting mediocre results. Exceptional people are always looking for ways to climb to the next level and beyond.

Look for ways to be excellent at work and at home. Look for opportunities to shine and don't whine.

A standard of personal and professional excellence doesn't mean you are trying to put anyone else down. It's not about being better than anyone else, but being better than *your* average. It's about being *your* best.

A commitment to excellence means continuously striving to improve. Excellence means you don't get comfortable with the status quo. Excellence means you do get comfortable being uncomfortable. Anytime we are striving for improvement, there will be some discomfort because growth requires us to stretch ourselves as we reach farther than we have in the past.

Excellence means over delivering.

When you over deliver, you will find your credibility and influence with others increases dramatically. But, you will also find your personal satisfaction increases. Your pride in the job you've done will increase dramatically too.

Many companies, people, and leaders settle for being average and dull. Just as shiny objects get noticed, so do shiny people. When you're excellent, you're also shiny.

CHAPTER 27
EXCELLENCE MEANS
GETTING RESULTS

"Quality is never an accident; it is always the result of high intention, sincere effort, intelligent direction and skillful execution; it represents the wise choice of many alternatives."

~ William A. Foster

As a speaker, being invited to give a TED/TEDx talk is an incredible honor. If you aren't familiar with TED/TEDx talks, they are short speeches designed to deliver an *"Idea Worth Spreading."*

Chris Andersen, Curator of TED Talks, says, *"Our ideas make us who we are. And, speakers who have figured out how to spread their ideas into others' minds are able to create ripple effects of untold consequence."*

It's an honor to be invited to share your own *"Idea Worth Spreading"* and it's a responsibility to deliver that idea in a compelling way that leaves the audience inspired.

When I first discovered TEDx talks, I decided right away I wanted to give one. I had a compelling story to share about leaving home at 19 after seven years of sexual abuse by my father. I knew my story was inspirational in some way to many people. I've realized my determination not to let the years of extreme sexual abuse hold me back from living a full and productive life today is inspiring to others.

I had a story of hardship and overcoming adversity after years of growing up in an abusive and dysfunctional home. I had a story of hard work after spending 10 years going to college, first to earn my GED and then to earn three college degrees with a cumulative 4.0 GPA while working full time or even sometimes two jobs. I also had a story of success after enjoying more than 10 years in the healthcare field where I eventually attained a high level position for a large healthcare organization.

The problem was I didn't have an idea worth

spreading.

As a speaker, it's not just about telling a story but sharing an idea or concept that will help the audience learn from your transformation and apply it to their own lives. We are inspired when we learn of others overcoming because it gives us hope for our own situation. But, I wasn't able to provide that inspiration until I was able to not only tell my story, but also help others understand how they could learn and benefit from my journey.

In 2013, I first started sharing my personal story of overcoming abuse. And honestly, I wasn't very good at it. But, I didn't let that stop me. I was determined to continue practicing, learning, and growing myself until I improved. I wanted to be excellent as a speaker, not because I wanted the recognition or applause, but because I realized it was my calling.

It's a worthy goal to want to be excellent at whatever we are doing. But, we must make sure we have mastered the foundational requirements before we can go on to deliver excellence.

In other words, we must learn to walk before we can learn to run.

I had to learn to get positive results by sharing my story in a way that helped others get results. At first, striving for excellence means getting results. Then, it means getting exceptional results.

In January 2014, I applied to give a TEDx talk. I applied many, many, times over the next three years. During those years, I practiced speaking every chance I had. I wrote what my TEDx talk would cover if I ever got the opportunity to give one and refined it word by word.

Then, I quit focusing on TEDx. I realized if I was changing lives when I spoke, it didn't matter if it was from a TEDx stage, a stage at a large conference, or a room with three women at a shelter.

I simply focused on getting results by helping others get results. And, I continued to try to improve.

In early 2017, an acquaintance reached out to me and suggested I apply to give a TEDx talk at an upcoming event in his area. I had moved that dream to the back burner, but I dusted it off, pulled out the script written more than two years before, and sent in an audition video. After dozens of rejections, I didn't put too much hope into the opportunity, but it wouldn't hurt to try. I had learned not to be disappointed when I wasn't accepted because it simply meant I wasn't ready. I sent the application off via email and forgot about it.

Excellence is about getting results and then getting exceptional results. I had learned how to get results and was working toward getting exceptional results.

Getting results is much like making sure you have gas in your car before you worry about how clean it is. It doesn't matter how shiny and polished your car is if you don't have any gas in the tank. You're not going anywhere.

First, make sure you've mastered the basics. Then, shift your focus to producing with excellence.

Four months after sending off my application, I received an email. *"Dear Ria: Our curating committee reviewed 179 applications from around the world. I am pleased to inform you, you are one of the 18 people who was selected to give a TEDx talk."*

On November 2, 2017, I took the stage in Wilmington, Delaware to deliver my *"Idea Worth Spreading."* You can watch it at: RiaStory.com/Tedx.

CHAPTER 28
EXCELLENCE MEANS GIVING AN EXTRA INCH

"There's only one real sin, and that is to persuade oneself that second best is anything but second best."
> ~ Doris Lessing

Take an extra few minutes to spell check a document, print it out, and read it. Re-read it before you pass it on to someone else. It's amazing how one last little glance before you call something complete will allow you to catch a mistake. It might be little or it might be big, but it will reflect the quality and the excellence of YOU.

Your standards for yourself need to be higher than anyone else's expectations of you. Excellence is doing something above and beyond what is normally considered acceptable. Be more than acceptable. Be exceptional.

I saw Rorke Denver, a former Navy Seal, speak at a Leadercast event several years ago. He said to everyone in the audience, *"Raise both hands as high as you can."* Instantly, everyone stuck both hands high up in the air. Then, he said, *"Raise them one inch higher."* Everyone was able to reach a little higher. Then, he said, *"Please give me just one inch more."* Nearly everyone sat up a little straighter and had another inch to give.

His point was that most of us often hold something back. We hold a *"reserve."* After we do as much as we think we can, we often realize we can still do more. We can and should learn to tap into that capacity without being asked.

Doing so will help you establish excellence in everything you do. Take the time to showcase, polish, proofread, and spell check every area of your life, not just some areas. Often, the little details are what will take you from mediocre to excellent and from average to exceptional.

That's important because, regardless of where you

work, you are always working for yourself. And, the reputation of *your* brand will be based on whether *you* deliver average or exceptional results.

My friend Amir Ghannad says, *"If you expect to have a six figure business, then provide seven figure service."*

Going the extra inch shows you are different and sets you apart from others because many people won't go an extra inch, much less an extra mile, even when asked.

I read a book by a very popular speaker and consultant with advice on building a very lucrative speaking and consulting business. But, one thing disappointed me. He suggested anytime you are hired as a speaker, you should refuse to do anything else. He specifically stated, speakers should be considered *"better than"* and shouldn't be asked to help move chairs or tables or perform any other task outside of delivering the speech itself. I was shocked. Refusing to help a client, when you can, is not an example of delivering seven figure service. It's not even two figure service in my opinion.

Whatever you're doing, customer service means delivering with excellence. If you work for someone, they are your number one customer. Provide excellent service and you will soon find your influence grows in leaps and bounds. If you are working for yourself, provide excellent service to your customers. You will find your business increases exponentially. If you are married, go above and beyond in the little things. You'll find your relationship strengthened immeasurably.

The perception of excellence is often in the details or the small things. Linda Kaplan Thaler and Robin Koval, authors of *The Power of Small*, stated, *"Our smallest actions and gestures often have outsized impact on our biggest goals. Going that extra inch, whether with a client, customer, family member, or friend, speaks volumes to others about our talent, personality, and motivations. After all, if we can't take care of the small details, how can we be counted on to deliver what matters?"*

I look for ways to do this at home. Take a moment to notice if the toothpaste container is nearly empty and replace it with the full one if so. Then, you aren't leaving your spouse searching for toothpaste.

Hold the door for someone, arrive a few minutes early to a client appointment, and offer a bonus when you can. By going just one inch farther than you have to, you'll discover there are many ways to ACHIEVE excellence.

I look for ways to do this with my clients. One coaching client paid for a coaching package with several hours of phone support. At the end of her paid hours, we had not reached the goal she wanted to achieve. Rather than simply tell her, *"Too bad,"* I met with her in person for several hours without an additional fee. Together, we worked through her project until she was satisfied. I'm not always able to deliver service like that, but anytime I add value above and beyond what is required and expected, I take the opportunity.

Successful people realize the value of becoming more valuable by adding more value. When you are willing to give more, do more, and be more in order to help others, you move beyond success and ACHIEVE significance.

The little things are the big things when it comes to people. Going the extra inch will take you the extra mile in life and leadership. It will also help you maximize your potential.

ACKNOWLEDGEMENTS

I'd like to thank my husband, Mack, for the feedback, synergy, ideas, proof-reading, editing, support, and for being my biggest cheerleader. And most of all, for helping me maximize *my* potential.

I want to thank the people in my life who inspire me, including those whose stories I shared in this book. Our lives are filled with Everyday Heroes, we simply have to learn to see them.

I'd like to thank everyone who has helped me learn over the years, both examples of what to do and what not to do.

Most of all, I want to thank God for the blessings and opportunities He has given me and for the hope of eternal salvation.

REFERENCES

Chapter Three:
1) Carey D. Lohrenz, *Fearless Leadership* (Greenleaf Book Group Press, 2014)
2) Carol Dweck, *Mindset: The New Psychology of Success* (Ballantine Books, 2006, 2016)

Chapter Fourteen:
1) Andy Stanley, *Like A Rock: Becoming A Person of Character* (Thomas Nelson Inc Publishers, 1997)

Chapter Fifteen:
1) New Year's Resolution Statistics, *Statistic Brain Research Institute* (https://www.statisticbrain.com/new-years-resolution-statistics/ retrieved July 13, 2018)

Chapter Twenty Two:
1) Ria Story, *PRIME Time: The Power of Effective Planning* (Top Story Leadership, LLC, 2016)
2) McChesney, Covey, & Huling, *The 4 Disciplines of Execution,* (Free Press, A division of Simon & Schuster, Inc., 2012)

Chapter Twenty Four:
1) John C. Maxwell, *No Limits: Blow the Cap off your Capacity* (Hatchette Book Group, 2017)

ABOUT THE AUTHOR

Like many, Ria faced adversity in life. Ria was sexually abused by her father from age 12 - 19, forced to play the role of his wife, and even shared with other men. Desperate to escape, she left home at 19 without a job, a car, or even a high school diploma. Ria learned to be resilient, not only surviving, but thriving. She worked her way through college, earning her MBA with a cumulative 4.0 GPA, and had a successful career in the corporate world of administrative healthcare.

Ria's background includes more than 10 years in administrative healthcare with several years in leadership and management including working as the Director of Compliance for a large healthcare organization. Ria's responsibilities included oversight of thousands of organizational policies, organizational compliance with all State and Federal regulations, and responsibility for several million dollars in Medicare appeals.

Today, Ria is a motivational leadership speaker, TEDx Speaker, and author of 10 books, including Leadership Gems for Women. Ria is a certified leadership speaker and trainer and was selected three times to speak on stage at International John Maxwell Certification Events. Motivational speaker Les Brown also invited Ria to share the stage with him in Los Angeles, CA.

Ria has a passion for health and wellness and is a certified group fitness instructor. She has completed several marathons and half-marathons and won both the Alabama and Georgia Women's State Mountain Biking Championships in 2011 and 2012.

Ria shares powerful leadership principles and tools of transformation from her journey to equip and empower women, helping them develop 360° influence and maximize their potential in life and leadership.

Order books online at Amazon or RiaStory.com

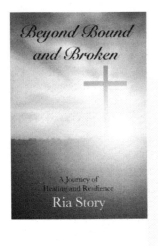

In *Beyond Bound and Broken,* Ria shares how she overcame the shame, fear, and doubt she developed after enduring years of extreme sexual abuse by her father. Forced to play the role of a wife and even shared with other men due to her father's perversions, Ria left home at 19 without a job, a car, or even a high-school diploma. This book also contains lessons on resilience and overcoming adversity that you can apply to your own life.

In *Ria's Story From Ashes To Beauty*, Ria tells her personal story of growing up as a victim of extreme sexual abuse from age 12 – 19, leaving home to escape, and her decision to tell her story

Order books online at Amazon or RiaStory.com

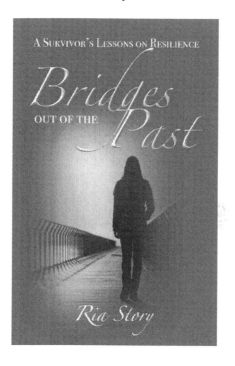

It's not what happens to you in life. It's who you become because of it. We all experience pain, grief, and loss in life. Resilience is the difference between *"I didn't die,"* and *"I learned to live again."* In this captivating book on resilience, Ria walks you through her own horrific story of more than seven years of sexual abuse by her father. She then shares how she learned not only to survive, but also to thrive in spite of her past. Learn how to overcome challenges, obstacles, and adversity in your own life by building a bridge out of the past and into the future.

(Watch 7 minutes of her story at RiaStory.com/TEDx)

Order books online at Amazon or RiaStory.com

Note: Leadership Gems is the generic, non-gender specific, version of Leadership Gems for Women. The content is very similar.

Women are naturally high impact leaders because they are relationship oriented. However, it's a *"man's world"* out there and natural ability isn't enough to help you be successful as a leader. You must be intentional.

Ria packed these books with 30 leadership gems which very successful people internalize and apply. Ria has combined her years of experience in leadership roles of different organizations along with years of studying, teaching, training, and speaking on leadership to give you these 30, short and simple, yet powerful and profound, lessons to help you become very successful, regardless of whether you are in a formal leadership position or not.

Order books online at Amazon or RiaStory.com

Become inspired by this 30-day collection of daily devotions for women, where you will find practical advice on intentionally living with a grateful heart, inspirational quotes, short journaling opportunities, and scripture from God's Word on practicing gratitude.

Order books online at Amazon or RiaStory.com

Ria's *Effective Leadership Series* books are written to develop and enhance your leadership skills, while also helping you increase your abilities in areas like communication and relationships, time management, planning and execution, leading and implementing change. Look for more books in the *Effective Leadership Series*:

- *Straight Talk: The Power of Effective Communication*

- *PRIME Time: The Power of Effective Planning*

- *Change Happens: Leading Yourself and Others through Change (Co-authored by Ria & Mack Story)*

- *Leadership Gems & Leadership Gems for Women*

Order books online at Amazon or TopStoryLeadership.com

High impact leaders align their habits with key values in order to maximize their influence. High impact leaders intentionally grow and develop themselves in an effort to more effectively grow and develop others. These *10 Values* are commonly understood. However, they are not always commonly practiced. These *10 Values* will help you build trust and accelerate relationship building. Those mastering these *10 Values* will be able to lead with speed as they develop 360° of influence from wherever they are.

Order books online at Amazon or TopStoryLeadership.com

Are you looking for transformation in your life? Do you want better results? Do you want stronger relationships?

In *Defining Influence*, Mack breaks down many of the principles that will allow anyone at any level to methodically and intentionally increase their positive influence.

Mack blends his personal growth journey with lessons on the principles he learned along the way. He's not telling you what he learned after years of research, but rather what he learned from years of application and transformation. Everything rises and falls on influence.

Order books online at Amazon or TopStoryLeadership.com

10 Foundational Elements of Intentional Transformation serves as a source of motivation and inspiration to help you climb your way to the next level and beyond as you learn to intentionally create a better future for yourself. The pages will ENCOURAGE, ENGAGE, and EMPOWER you as you become more focused and intentional about moving from where you are to where you want to be.

All of us are somewhere, but most of us want to be somewhere else. However, we don't always know how to get there. You will learn how to intentionally move forward as you learn to navigate the 10 foundational layers of transformation.

Order books online at Amazon or TopStoryLeadership.com

"Sales persuasion and influence, moving others, has changed more in the last 10 years than it has in the last 100 years. It has transitioned from buyer beware to seller beware" ~ Daniel Pink

So, it's no longer *"Buyer beware!"* It's *"Seller beware!"* Why? Today, the buyer has the advantage over the seller. Most often, they are holding it in their hand. It's a smart phone. They can learn everything about your product before they meet you. They can compare features and prices instantly. The major advantage you do still have is: YOU! IF they like you. IF they trust you. IF they feel you want to help them. This book is filled with 30 short chapters providing unique insights that will give you the advantage, not over the buyer, but over your competition: those who are selling what you're selling. It will help you sell yourself.

Order books online at Amazon or BlueCollarLeadership.com

Are you ready to play at the next level and beyond?

In today's high stakes game of business, the players on the team are the competitive advantage for any organization. But, only if they are on the field instead of on the bench.

The competitive advantage for every individual is developing 360° of influence regardless of position, title, or rank.

Blue-Collar Leadership® & *Teamwork* provides a simple, yet powerful and unique, resource for individuals who want to increase their influence and make a high impact. It's also a resource and tool for leaders, teams, and organizations, who are ready to Engage the Front Line to Improve the Bottom Line.

Order books online at Amazon or BlueCollarLeadership.com

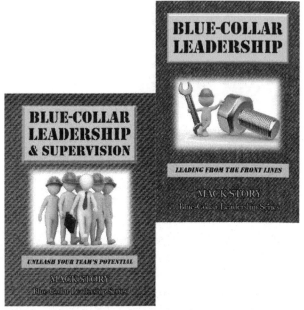

"I wish someone had given me these books 30 years ago when I started my career on the front lines. They would have changed my life then. They can change your life now." ~ Mack Story

Blue-Collar Leadership® & Supervision and *Blue-Collar Leadership®* are written specifically for those who lead the people on the frontlines and for those on the front lines. With 30 short, easy to read 3 page chapters, these books contain powerful, yet simple to understand leadership lessons.

Down load the first 5 chapters of each book FREE at: BlueCollarLeadership.com

Order books online at Amazon or BlueCollarLeadership.com

The biggest challenge in process improvement and cultural transformation isn't identifying the problems. It's execution: implementing and sustaining the solutions.

Blue-Collar Kaizen is a resource for anyone in any position who is, or will be, leading a team through process improvement and change. Learn to engage, empower, and encourage your team for long term buy-in and sustained gains.

Mack Story has over 11,000 hours experience leading hundreds of leaders and thousands of their cross-functional kaizen team members through process improvement, organizational change, and cultural transformation.

Order books online at Amazon or TopStoryLeadership.com

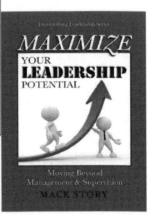

"I wish someone had given me these books 30 years ago when I started my career. They would have changed my life then. They can change your life now." ~ Mack Story

MAXIMIZE Your Potential will help you learn to lead yourself well. *MAXIMIZE Your Leadership Potential* will help you learn to lead others well. With 30 short, easy to read 3 page chapters, these books contain simple and easy to understand, yet powerful leadership lessons.

Note: These two MAXIMIZE books are the white-collar, or non-specific, version of the Blue-Collar Leadership® books and contain nearly identical content.

Made in the USA
Columbia, SC
14 December 2018